Curiosities Series

Nevada CURIOSITIES

Quirky characters,
roadside oddities &
other offbeat stuff

Richard Moreno

gpp®

Guilford, Connecticut

To buy books in quantity for corporate use
or incentives, call **(800) 962-0973**
or e-mail **premiums@GlobePequot.com.**

gpp

Text design by Bret Kerr
Layout by Melissa Evarts
Maps by Daniel Lloyd © Morris Book Publishing, LLC

Photos courtesy of Richard Moreno, unless otherwise credited.

Library of Congress Cataloging-in-Publication Data is available on file.

ISBN 978-0-7627-4682-8

Printed in the United States of America
10 9 8 7 6 5 4 3 2 1

To my friend and partner, Pam. Thanks for everything you do.

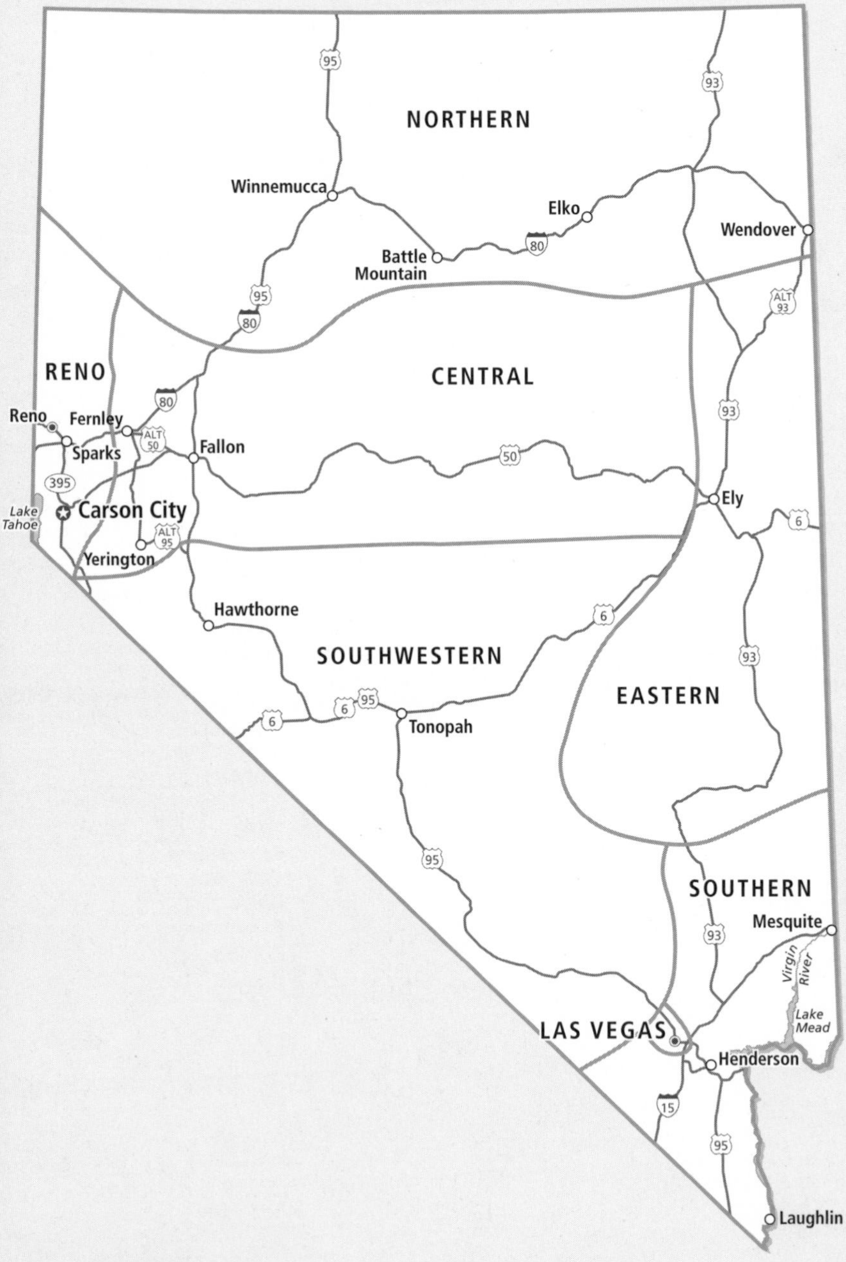

Nevada Overview

contents

introduction

Nevada is Maureen Stapleton in the 1978 Woody Allen film *Interiors*. It's a place that's just a little bit louder than it ought to be, a little bit brighter than it needs to be, and, perhaps, a little bit less cultured than it wants to be. It's a curious mixture of liberal attitude—it's the only state with legal prostitution and was the first state to legalize gambling—and populist conservatism—it is the home of the "Sagebrush Rebellion," a movement to turn control of government-supervised public lands over to private hands.

Years ago, I moved to Nevada with the expectation that I would stay there for only a short time. But something happened. I began to like Nevada. I learned how to pronounce its name (Nuh-va-duh) like a Nevadan and learned that even though the town of Verdi was named after the Italian composer, its name isn't pronounced like his name (it's Ver-dye, Nuh-va-duh). And then there's the way Nevadans say Genoa, a town named after the Italian city of the same name but also pronounced differently.

I discovered that Nevada does things its own—some might say, curious—way. For example, one of the state's most popular museums isn't some musty storehouse of dinosaur bones or ancient marble statues of forgotten figures; it's one devoted to the life of a flamboyant piano player who wore red, white, and blue rhinestone hot pants. One of the most popular sights on a lonely highway that spans the center of the state is a giant cottonwood tree filled with hundreds of pairs of shoes. When the minister in one of the oldest churches in the state wants to ring the bell announcing services, he's got to stand on top of a toilet seat to reach the bell rope. And there's a dirt road in a remote northern corner of the state lined with large boulders that have been carved with fortune cookie–type sayings like "The human race is like a watch; it takes all the parts to make it work" and "The time we enjoy wasting is not wasted time."

Nevada's State Bush

Nevada's state flower is a scruffy shrub. Unlike many states, which have beautiful flowers like roses or camellias as their official floral species, Nevada's flower is a fragrant, green-gray plant formally known as *Artemisia tridentata.* Technically, it is a member of the wormwood family. It can grow up to 12 feet high, seems to survive in the most inhospitable of places, and serves as an important winter food for cattle and sheep.

Although sagebrush is found nearly everywhere in the state, it is not exactly beloved. Onetime Nevadan Mark Twain described it as the "fag-end of vegetable creation" and wrote that "when crushed, sagebrush emits an odor which isn't exactly magnolia and equally isn't polecat—but it is a sort of compromise between the two." He also called it only a "fair" fuel and claimed that nothing could abide its flavor save "the jackass and his illegitimate child the mule." Comedian Johnny Carson was once so amused by the fact that Nevada's state flower was a bush that he held up a scraggly cluster of sagebrush branches and asked his audience to imagine sending a bouquet to a wife or girlfriend for Valentine's Day.

On the other hand, author Robert Laxalt, who spent nearly his entire life in Nevada, felt far more kindly toward the shrub. He wrote of being abroad when he received a letter from his daughter. Inside the pages of her note was "a single sprig of Nevada sagebrush. Before I could protect myself, the memories were summoned up and washed over me in a flood."

It smelled like home.

introduction

Nevada fascinated me, and I ended up spending more than a quarter of a century exploring all that it had to offer. I found that the more I learned about the state, the more it became my kind of place. I've done my best to share some of the quirkiest, funniest, and most fascinating stories that I've learned about the Silver State. None of this would have been possible without assistance, including from Nevada State Archivist Guy Louis Rocha and his wonderful "Myth of the Month" column (www.nevadaculture.org/docs/nsla/archives/myth/) as well as the archives of the *Reno Gazette-Journal, Las Vegas Review-Journal, Las Vegas Sun,* and *Nevada Magazine*. Special thanks also to my patient wife, Pam, and my two wonderful children, Hank and Julia. And a big thanks to Margaret Ann Schneweis, who suggested this in the first place.

I hope you enjoy.

CHAPTER

1

Las Vegas
Nevada's City of Lights

"In the case of an earthquake hitting Las Vegas, be sure to go straight to the Keno Lounge. Nothing ever gets hit there."

—Old joke

It is ironic *that Las Vegas was originally settled by Mormons, who, as a general rule, don't smoke, drink, gamble, or even have coffee. In 1855 thirty Mormon missionaries from Salt Lake City established the first settlement in the Las Vegas Valley. The plan was to convert the local Native Americans into Latter-Day Saints and set up a rest stop for travelers heading between Utah and southern California.*

But, like a lot of Las Vegas dreams, it quickly faded. The Las Vegas Mission, which later became known as the Old Mormon Fort, survived for about two years—or about as long as the musical Spamalot *lasted at the Wynn Las Vegas resort.*

A few years later, the abandoned mission evolved into a successful ranch that catered to tired and thirsty desert travelers. In the early twentieth century, the ranch became a railroad stop, and the seeds of the modern town of Las Vegas were planted.

Flash-forward about half a century, when gangster Benjamin "Bugsy" Siegel has just purchased a piece of the Flamingo Hotel and starts talking up Vegas as the new Miami. Although he didn't live long enough to see his dream become a reality, his vision helped transform the sleepy desert town into a gambling mecca.

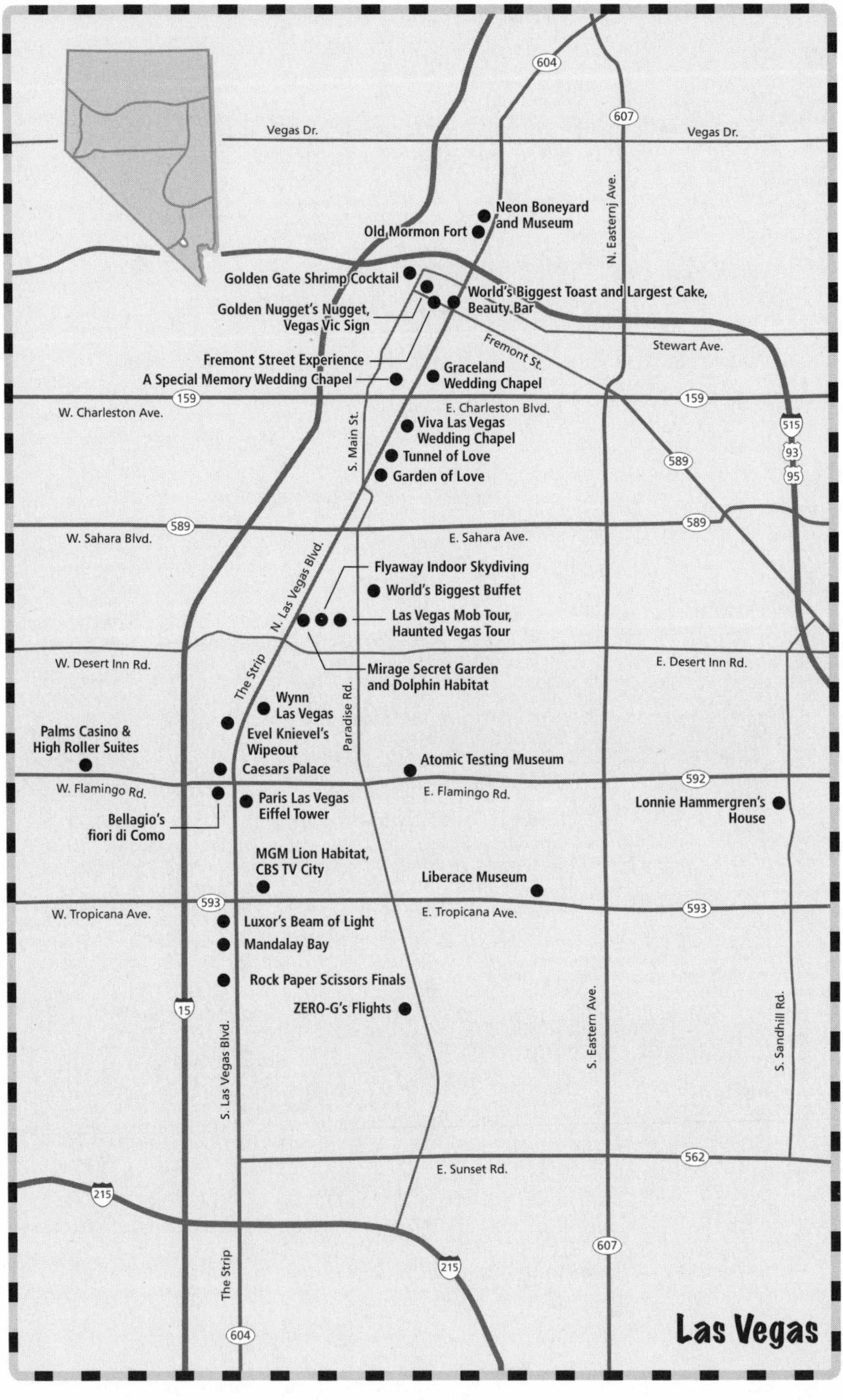
Las Vegas
Vegas Dr.
Vegas Dr.
604
607
Neon Boneyard and Museum
Old Mormon Fort
N. Easternj Ave.
Golden Gate Shrimp Cocktail
World's Biggest Toast and Largest Cake, Beauty Bar
Golden Nugget's Nugget, Vegas Vic Sign
Fremont St.
Stewart Ave.
Fremont Street Experience
A Special Memory Wedding Chapel
Graceland Wedding Chapel
159
W. Charleston Ave.
E. Charleston Blvd.
159
515
93
95
Viva Las Vegas Wedding Chapel
S. Main St.
Tunnel of Love
Garden of Love
589
589
W. Sahara Blvd.
E. Sahara Ave.
589
N. Las Vegas Blvd.
Flyaway Indoor Skydiving
World's Biggest Buffet
Las Vegas Mob Tour, Haunted Vegas Tour
W. Desert Inn Rd.
E. Desert Inn Rd.
Mirage Secret Garden and Dolphin Habitat
The Strip
Wynn Las Vegas
Paradise Rd.
Palms Casino & High Roller Suites
Evel Knievel's Wipeout
Caesars Palace
Atomic Testing Museum
W. Flamingo Rd.
E. Flamingo Rd.
592
Lonnie Hammergren's House
Paris Las Vegas Eiffel Tower
Bellagio's fiori di Como
MGM Lion Habitat, CBS TV City
Liberace Museum
593
W. Tropicana Ave.
E. Tropicana Ave.
593
Luxor's Beam of Light
Mandalay Bay
Rock Paper Scissors Finals
ZERO-G's Flights
15
S. Las Vegas Blvd.
S. Eastern Ave.
S. Sandhill Rd.
E. Sunset Rd.
562
215
215
607
The Strip
604

So, even though the Mormon mission was a flop nearly a century earlier, it did prove one thing—don't forget to include a casino if you plan to make it in Las Vegas.

Las Vegas Does Have a History

There is something in Vegas that has been around longer than Wayne Newton. One of the original buildings of the Old Mormon Fort, the city's first settlement, can be found a few blocks north of downtown Las Vegas. Now a historic state park, the structure dates to 1855, although it has been changed and remodeled several times over the years.

Where it all began in Vegas—the Old Mormon Fort.

In 1929 it was leased and renovated by the Bureau of Reclamation for use as a lab during the construction of Hoover Dam. The rectangular adobe structure now houses a small museum featuring displays and exhibits detailing the fort's history. Additionally, one of the rooms contains nineteenth-century furnishings—not originals—that show how the building most likely looked near the turn of the twentieth century.

The park also contains reconstructions of the fort's north and south walls, one of the bastions, the corrals, and a replica of the Pioneer Garden, complete with various crops like those planted 150 years ago.

The Old Las Vegas Mormon Fort State Historic Park is located at 500 East Washington Avenue in Las Vegas, adjacent to Cashman Field and across the street from the Sawyer State Office Building. The park is open daily from 8:00 a.m. to 5:00 p.m. For information call (702) 486-3511.

Cold War Reminder: The Atomic Testing Museum

In the 1950s getting bombed in Nevada didn't always involve alcohol. Between 1951 and 1992 nearly 1,000 nuclear explosions were detonated at the Nevada Test Site, located 65 miles north of Las Vegas. The first test, nicknamed "Able," involved a B-50D Bomber dropping a nuclear device from an altitude of 19,700 feet onto a barren patch of desert known as "Frenchman Flat."

The subsequent explosion generated a brilliant ball of rose-colored fire, followed by a blue-purple afterglow for a few seconds and a small, yellow-brown cloud that slowly drifted away until it was dissipated by the winds.

During the next four decades, the 1,375-square-mile test site (larger than Rhode Island and one of the largest restricted areas in the United States) hosted hundreds of nuclear detonations. In the early years the nuclear blasts generated enormous mushroom-shaped

Photo courtesy of the Atomic Testing Museum

The Atomic Testing Museum shows how Nevada's state flower was once the mushroom cloud.

clouds that rose high into the sky. Watching the scheduled tests developed into a popular tourist attraction in Las Vegas. After 1962 the tests were moved underground as a result of growing concern about fallout from the clouds.

In 2005 the Atomic Testing Museum opened in Las Vegas. The 8,000-square-foot facility, an affiliate of the Smithsonian Institution, is one of the first public museums devoted to the impacts of the cold war.

Inside, state-of-the-art displays describe the role that the Nevada Test Site had in the development of nuclear weapons and the impact that "the bomb" had on American life.

Wandering through the museum, visitors can trace the development of the atomic bomb, including a copy of a letter from Albert Einstein urging President Franklin Roosevelt to investigate the use of atomic technology because the Germans were already researching ways to develop nuclear weapons.

In Ground Zero Theater, visitors can sit in a darkened room to watch a film about the history of the site and experience a leg-shaking simulation of an atmospheric nuclear test—except without the bothersome radiation.

Museum docents are often retired test site workers, who earnestly guide visitors through the galleries, which feature audio and video displays, genuine test site artifacts, and items illustrating the public fascination with atomic tests during the 1950s (check out the Kix cereal box promoting the "Kix Atomic Bomb Ring").

You could say this museum is a real blast.

The Atomic Testing Museum is located at 755 East Flamingo Road. Admission is $10 for adults; $7 for seniors, military, and youth (seven to seventeen). Children under six are admitted free. The museum is open Monday through Saturday, 9:00 a.m. to 5:00 p.m.; Sunday, 1:00 to 5:00 p.m.

A Real Glass Ceiling: The Bellagio Resort's *Fiori di Como*

If you wander into a typical hotel, the most impressive thing you might see over your head is either a grand chandelier or, in some of the places I've stayed, some dust and a nicely woven spiderweb.

At Las Vegas's Bellagio Resort, however, the ceiling above the hotel lobby is literally a work of art. Look up and you'll view the world's largest glass sculpture. Called *Fiori di Como,* which means "Flowers of Como," it was created by famed glass sculptor Dale Chihuly for the resort's original owner, Steve Wynn. The title reflects the fact that the Bellagio was inspired by the hotel on Lake Como in Italy.

Fiori di Como incorporates more than 2,000 handblown flowers in an eruption of vivid colors. Standing beneath the work is mesmerizing—each flower appears to be different and unique not only in color but also in size and shape.

Completed in 1998, the sculpture measures 65 feet 7 inches by 29 feet 6 inches (about 2,100 square feet) and weighs a staggering 40,000 pounds. Chihuly supervised a team of more than a hundred glassblowers, installers, and fabricators to build the piece.

The Seattle-based artist says that the most difficult part about crafting *Fiori di Como* was that everything about it had to be made from scratch. Nothing of that size and scale had ever been attempted before, so he had to develop new techniques for assembling and suspending the sculpture.

"It took about 10,000 pounds of steel for the armature and some 40,000 pounds of handblown glass—over 2,000 pieces positioned 15 to 25 feet overhead," he said. "It also demanded an entirely new type of hardware to attach the glass to the structure."

The massive glass artwork reportedly cost more than a million dollars, and today, according to at least one arts writer, it is probably worth at least eight times that amount.

But it's free to look at.

Photo courtesy of MGM Grand Mirage

The Bellagio's *Fiori di Como* colorful ceiling is the world's largest glass sculpture.

If you're impressed enough to want to take home a piece of Chihuly art, the Bellagio conveniently has the Chihuly Gallery, where visitors can purchase original works as well as books and videos about the artist.

The Bellagio is also home to the largest number of water fountains in the world, with more than 1,200 spraying jets on an 8.5-acre man-made lake in front of the resort. The choreographed, dancing fountains, which perform several times a day, can fire streams of water up to 460 feet into the air in time to music and lights. The fountains made a memorable star turn at the conclusion of the 2001 film *Ocean's Eleven*.

The 13,500-square-foot Bellagio Conservatory is another of the hotel's marvels. Displays inside the giant glass enclosure, which is free to tour, are changed five times a year—once for each of the four seasons and once for the Chinese New Year. Every time the display is changed, completely different plants and trees are installed, and a brand-new theme is presented. It is estimated that the hotel's 140 horticultural staff members spend an average of seven days, working around the clock, to change each display.

Kid Stuff for Grown-ups: The USA Rock Paper Scissors Finals

The old children's game of rock-paper-scissors, also known as RoShamBo, has hit the big time in Las Vegas. Once merely an amusing way for kids to either pass time or resolve differences, the venerable hand game is now the subject of a national tournament.

In 2006 the Mandalay Bay Resort hosted the inaugural USA Rock Paper Scissors Bud Light Finals. This competition, which was televised on the A&E cable network, attracted 260 of the best rock-paper-scissors players in the country, who competed for a $50,000 first prize.

The rules for playing the game are simple: Two contestants face off and at the count of three present either a fist (rock), a flat hand (paper), or two fingers (scissors). Paper beats rock, rock beats scissors, and scissors beats paper.

After nearly seven hours of flying hand gestures, the inaugural tournament winner was David McGill, a thirty-year-old "professional student" from Omaha, Nebraska, who managed to outlast all the other competitors.

Interestingly, the USA Rock Paper Scissors Bud Light Finals isn't the only such tournament in the country. There are actually two national sanctioning organizations for this former kids' game.

The oldest of the leagues is the World Rock Paper Scissors Society, based in Toronto, Canada. The American upstart is the USA Rock Paper Scissors group, created by Hollywood producer Matti Leshem with financial support from Anheuser-Busch.

At the kickoff event, many contestants apparently spent as much time thinking of what to wear to the event as they did in practicing their skills or developing strategy. A large number of the participants dressed in wacky and crazy costumes, ranging from a couple decked out as hot dog condiments to clones of Edward Scissorhands.

Not surprisingly given the main sponsor, most of the competitors consumed large quantities of beer during (as well as before and after) play.

If you feel like trying your hand at this age-old hand-gesturing game, the USARPS Web site (www.usarps.com) invites all comers to sign up for regional tourneys that lead to the big throwdown in Las Vegas, held each June. Better start practicing now.

A Bar That's Strictly BYOB (Bring Your Own Brush)

A decade ago, East Coast restaurateur and bar owner Paul Devitt opened the first Beauty Bar in a former beauty salon in New York City. Sporting a kitschy-retro beauty shop decor, the Manhattan nightclub became an instant hit by offering cosmetology-themed cocktails along with shampoos and manicures. Since then, the Beauty Bar concept has spread to other cities, including San Francisco, Los Angeles, San Diego, Austin, and Las Vegas.

The trendy Beauty Bar in downtown Las Vegas is the only place in town offering a manicure on the rocks.

Sin City's version is a bit different from its sister clubs in that it does not include an actual working beauty salon. Apparently, the Nevada State Board of Cosmetology has a rule that bans the selling of alcoholic beverages along with haircuts. As a result, Vegas's Beauty Bar offers nightly, free nail-care demonstrations.

Despite the fact that it's not a real clip joint, Beauty Bar has all the trappings. The club's classic 1950s hair salon appearance, including the overstuffed waiting room couches, reflects the fact that much of its interior was originally part of the Capri Salon of Beauty in Trenton, New Jersey. Additionally, the bullet-shaped hair dryers and orange-paneled alcove lights are from the now-demolished Algiers Hotel in Las Vegas.

Voted "Best Hipster Bar" in *Las Vegas Life* magazine, Beauty Bar caters to the twenty- and thirtysomething clubbers with its nightly mix of live deejay-spun sounds and creatively concocted beverages, such as the "Prell" (UV Vodka, Midori, and pineapple juice), "Blue Rinse" (UV Raspberry, sweet and sour, and chambord), the "Shampoo" (Jose Cuervo tequila, sweet and sour, triple sec, lime juice, and chambord), and the "Conditioner" (Stoli Vanilla, ginger ale, and lime juice).

Beauty Bar is located at 517 Fremont in downtown Las Vegas (702-598-1965). It's open Saturday, Sunday, and Tuesday, 9:00 p.m. to 4:00 a.m., and Wednesday through Friday, 5:00 p.m. to 4:00 a.m. There is no cover charge and—surprise—no gambling.

One to Chew On: The World's BIGGEST Buffet

It was a match made in gastronomic heaven—have one of the world's best-known brands of heartburn and indigestion relief products sponsor the world's largest buffet. On March 28, 2006, Alka Seltzer celebrated its seventy-fifth year of soothing upset tummies by sponsoring a 510-item buffet at the Las Vegas Hilton. The all-you-can-eat extravaganza, which set a Guinness World Record, included Mongolian chicken, salmon Wellington, cheese quesadillas, fajitas, barbecue beef ribs, fried chicken, tandoori chicken, soba noodle salad, bourbon-glazed ham, beef tenderloin tips braised in red wine, wood-roasted chicken breasts, tiramisu, New York–style cheesecake, and German chocolate cake.

Some twenty chefs and sous-chefs were on hand to present the dishes, which were accented by giant ice sculptures, including one spelling out a huge "75," as well as an array of bubbling columns and other effervescent decor. George Bargisen, the Las Vegas Hilton's executive director of culinary operations, who planned the menu and coordinated the event, said that his staff prepared 40 different soups; 149 types of desserts; 149 cold appetizers, salads, and sandwiches; and 152 hot items. In addition, there were ten carving stations to slice off slabs of roast beef, ham, and turkey and five "action" stations, which were serving areas that prepared individualized servings of various pastas and desserts.

Open to the public, the event attracted 848 diners, each of whom paid $7.50 for the opportunity to overindulge their way into history. All proceeds were donated to America's Second Harvest, the largest charitable hunger-relief organization in the United States.

Actress and comedian Kathy Griffin—who took the first bite—hosted the food fest, which was held in one of the Hilton's largest ballrooms. The orgy of culinary offerings covered more than 500 feet of combined table surface, spread across the 140-foot length of the room.

"Let's face it. I'm going to overindulge today. I'm going to pop a couple of Alka Seltzer and then I'm going to be fine," Griffin joked during an interview just before the first forks were raised.

Fortunately for those who couldn't believe they ate the whole thing, Alka Seltzer had relief stations scattered throughout the room. Plop, plop, fizz, fizz. Oh, what a relief it is.

Downtown Las Vegas's Electronic Lid

It's essentially the world's biggest TV screen. Officially known as the Fremont Street Experience, it is a 1,462-foot-long, rounded canopy that spreads over a 5-block section of Fremont Street in downtown Las Vegas. It stands 90 feet high, is 5 feet deep, and has a curved radius of 44 feet. Its interior surface covers more than 175,000 square feet (about 4 acres), and it has 12.5 million energy-efficient, synchronized red, blue, and green light-emitting diodes (LEDs). It was constructed in 1995 for about $70 million and was upgraded in 2004 at a cost of $17 million.

The covering serves to create a pedestrian mall on Fremont Street, once a popular cruising boulevard but now closed to auto traffic. Ten casinos, including Fitzgerald's, the Golden Nugget, and the Four Queens, are tucked inside the canopy, which creates the feeling that the downtown is one huge gaming mall.

Photo courtesy of the Las Vegas Convention and Visitors Authority

Downtown Las Vegas's Fremont Street Experience is the world's largest TV screen—and it makes a great umbrella.

But it's not just the size or the cost that makes the Fremont Street Experience a must-see attraction. About once an hour, between dusk and midnight, the ceiling transforms into the world's largest light-and-music show. Backed by 550,000 watts of sound pumping through more than 200 speakers, the roof erupts in a colorful graphic presentation called "Viva Vision" that combines computer animation, music, and special lighting effects. The light-and-music selections vary during the year but can include such productions as *The Drop,* a mystical underwater journey; *Area 51,* an otherworldly light-and-sound show; and *American Freedom,* a patriotic salute with classic images of Americana.

The free performances last six to eight minutes, and afterward the surrounding casino lights return along with soft ambient music. One impact of the canopy is that it has helped transform downtown Las Vegas into a busy place no matter what time of the day or night.

Adjacent to the Fremont Street Experience is Neonopolis, a $100 million, 250,000-square-foot open-air retail and office complex. While still trying to attract tenants, Neonopolis does have a bowling alley, a fourteen-screen movie facility, restaurants, fast-food outlets, bars, and souvenir shops.

The Fremont Street Experience is located on Fremont Street between Main and Fourth Streets in downtown Las Vegas.

"Howdy, Pardner"

Since 1951 the massive neon and metal cowboy named Vegas Vic has greeted visitors to downtown Las Vegas. Standing 40 feet tall, the illuminated buckaroo weighs about six tons and, at the time it was erected on top of the Pioneer Club in downtown Las Vegas, was the world's largest mechanical sign (his arm waved, his eye winked, and his cigarette moved and blew smoke rings). Vic, who wears a cowboy hat and boots, blue jeans, a yellow checked shirt, and a red bandanna, was designed by Patrick Denner of the Young Electric Sign Company (YESCO). Denner also created Wendover Will, a 63-foot neon cowboy clone built in 1952 for the State Line Casino in West Wendover.

The design of Vegas Vic was based on an image that the Las Vegas Chamber of Commerce began using in the late 1940s, when the city was promoting itself with the slogan "Still a Frontier Town" (a far cry from Sin City's more recent "What Happens Here, Stays Here" advertisements).

In the mid-1950s Vic began greeting passersby with a booming "Howdy, pardner" message that was broadcast every fifteen minutes. According to local legend, in 1966 actors Lee Marvin and Woody Strode were staying in the nearby Mint Hotel during the filming

For more than a half century, the neon cowboy called Vegas Vic has welcomed visitors to Glitter Gulch.

of *The Professionals* and complained that Vic's voice was annoying them. The owners of the Pioneer Club removed his voice box and didn't replace it for more than two decades (Vic, however, went silent again in the 1990s—maybe it was all those years of smoking neon cigarettes).

The 1990s weren't a good time for the giant neon cowhand. By 1991 he had stopped waving his arm, supposedly because the Pioneer Club's owner at the time didn't like how it looked. In addition, in 1994 the construction of the Fremont Street Experience, a massive electronic canopy erected over several downtown Las Vegas blocks, necessitated the trimming of Vic's cowboy hat, which was chopped by a few feet. In January 2000 the *Las Vegas Review-Journal* reported, "Vic is in poor shape now. Only half of his body, including one of his two eyes, lights up at night. His waving arm hasn't worked in years. His colorful clothes have faded and peeled."

Fortunately, later that year Vic was given a long-overdue renovation. His sheet metal was repainted, mechanical parts were repaired, and neon tubing was patched and refilled with the electrified gases that give him his special glow.

Over his first half century, Vic has become one of Las Vegas's most endearing symbols. He has been described by *VIA* magazine as "Mr. Vegas" and has appeared in countless TV commercials, music videos, and TV shows, as well as in films such as *The Amazing Colossal Man, Viva Las Vegas, Diamonds Are Forever,* and *Casino*.

Vegas Vic can be seen standing atop the now-closed Pioneer Club (now a souvenir shop) at 25 East Fremont Street.

No Scrimping on *This* Shrimp

With the advent of splashy megaresorts, ultra-exclusive dance clubs, pricey shopping malls, and overpriced gourmet restaurants, some old-timers lament the passing of the "old" Las Vegas, with its bargain buffets and two-for-one keno. Fortunately for them, there's still one place that hasn't changed much during the past half century—the

Golden Gate Hotel and Casino in downtown Las Vegas. Since 1959 the small hotel-casino's deli has served a scoop of cold-water bay shrimp swimming in a thick, red homemade cocktail sauce with a wedge of lemon for less than a buck. Originally 50 cents, the price of the Golden Gate's shrimp cocktail increased to 99 cents in 1991 and to $1.99 in 2008.

When in Vegas, make sure to stop at the Golden Gate Hotel, home of the famous $1.99 shrimp cocktail—the city's best bargain.

The tangy seafood concoction is served in a tulip cocktail glass with crackers. The hotel reports that it goes through nearly two tons of shrimp per week (54 pounds of big shrimp and 217 pounds of bay shrimp per day) and has sold more than thirty million shrimp cocktails since the promotion began.

Of course, part of the charm of picking up a shrimp cocktail is checking out the Golden Gate. The historic hotel dates to 1905, when the San Pedro, Los Angeles, and Salt Lake Railroad auctioned sites for the community that would become Las Vegas. The lot on the corner of Fremont and Main Streets was purchased for $1,750, and within a year a small hotel and casino opened, known as the Hotel Nevada. The property had Las Vegas's first telephone (and phone number: #1) and, in 1931, received air-conditioning and a new name, the Sal Sagev (*Las Vegas* spelled backwards).

In the mid-1950s a group of San Francisco investors purchased the venerable hotel, renamed it the Golden Gate, and began serving those famous shrimp cocktails. In the 1990s the hotel was restored to its 1930s appearance.

Some Nugget

It just makes sense that if you have a hotel-casino and call it the Golden Nugget, you ought to have at least one golden nugget. The Golden Nugget hotel-casino in downtown Las Vegas did just that—except that its nugget is a staggering 875-troy-ounce hunk of gold (about 61 pounds 11 ounces), the largest gold nugget on public display in the world.

Called "The Hand of Faith" because of its glovelike shape, the Golden Nugget's golden nugget was uncovered near Wedderburn, Victoria, Australia, in October 1980. It was found about 6 inches below the ground in a vertical position by a man using a metal detector. According to the Golden Nugget, "The Hand of Faith" is worth more than $425,000. As an aside, the largest gold nugget ever recorded was a 172-pound specimen, known as the "Welcome Stranger"; it was found in 1869, also in Victoria, Australia. It was melted down and produced about 156 pounds of pure gold.

Visitors to the Golden Nugget, located on Fremont Street, can view "The Hand of Faith" in the hotel's lobby. The Golden Nugget traces its roots to 1946, when it became the first building in Sin City erected specifically for gambling. In 1973 Steve Wynn took over the aging property and transformed it from a Victorian/frontier-themed grind-joint to a more classical hotel with lots of marble and shiny brass. More recently, it has been purchased by the Landry Restaurants chain (owners of Landry's Seafood House, Rainforest Café, Chart House, and others), which remodeled the rooms, casino areas, and public space (including "The Hand of Faith" display); added a giant pool with an aquarium; revamped several restaurants; and announced plans for another hotel tower.

Where Old Neon Goes to Die

Think of the Las Vegas Neon Museum and its Neon Boneyard as a retirement home for old electric and neon signs. Many marquees and lighted signs end up in the junkyard, but a few are salvaged—some even restored—to become part of the Neon Museum or the Neon Boneyard, as the museum's storage area is known.

The Neon Museum is actually an outdoor display area at the entrance to the Fremont Street Experience in downtown Las Vegas. It contains eleven restored, historic Las Vegas signs, including the Hacienda Horse and Rider, originally installed at the Hacienda Hotel in 1967; Aladdin's Lamp, a giant neon, fairy tale–style lamp erected in 1966 in front of the Aladdin Hotel; the cartoony Andy Anderson neon mascot, which in 1956 was placed in front of the local Anderson Dairy; and the Chief Hotel Court sign, which was installed around 1940 at a former downtown Las Vegas hotel.

Future plans call for the museum to have a visitor center, housed in the restored lobby of the historic La Concha Motel. The facil-

The place where old neon is put out to pasture—Las Vegas's Neon Museum's Boneyard.

ity will sit at the entrance to the three-acre Boneyard at the north end of Las Vegas Boulevard (821 Las Vegas Boulevard North) near Cashman Center. In 2006 the La Concha's 1,000-foot lobby was dismantled and painstakingly moved from the southern end of the Las Vegas Strip to the Boneyard. The structure, which boasts a futuristic, swooping, shell-shaped roof, was built in 1961 and was designed by noted African-American architect Paul Revere Williams, who was also responsible for the Beverly Hills Hotel and the United Nations Building in Paris. It is considered a prime example of the mid-twentieth-century modern roadside "Googie" style of architecture.

The Boneyard, which is open only by appointment, offers an opportunity to wander through the oversize skeletons of many of

Las Vegas's most recognizable signs, including the Binion's Horseshoe marquee, the high-heeled women's shoe that once topped the Silver Slipper Casino, and a curved Golden Nugget entrance sign. All are in various states of disrepair, but the museum hopes to restore many of these icons sometime in the future. Most were built by the Young Electric Sign Company (YESCO), which leased them to the establishments but retained ownership. When the signs were no longer wanted or needed, YESCO stored them for many years on its own property. A few years ago, they were relocated to the museum's site. Tours of the Boneyard are available for groups of ten or more ($5 per person) or for smaller groups (minimum donation of $50). To submit a tour request go to the museum's Web site at www.neonmuseum.org.

When a Shake Just Isn't Enough

Once upon a time, the most expensive thing you could do with a burger was to add cheese and french fries. However, several Las Vegas resorts have decided to reconfigure the lowly hamburger meal into something more. At the Mandalay Bay's Fleur de Lys restaurant, diners can order the world's most expensive burger experience. The Fleur Burger 5000, concocted by Chef Hubert Keller, is made of Kobe beef, served on a brioche truffle bun, and topped with foie gras, black truffles, and Keller's secret truffle sauce—for a mere $5,000. It does come with a beverage, a bottle of Chateau Petrus 1990, which is poured into Ichendorf Brunello stemware from Italy, which will be mailed to your home after your meal. The meal without the wine is a mere $75.

Not to outdone, the trendy Palms Casino boasts the world's most expensive combo meal: Carl's Jr.'s Six Dollar Burger with fries and a bottle of 1982 Chateau Petrus Pomerol Bordeaux for $6,000. This pricey "value" meal is available only on the room service menu. The deal here is that a bottle of Chateau Petrus—one of Dr. Hannibal Lecter's favorite wines in the Thomas Harris novels—usually costs $6,000, so the Palms is tossing in the burger and fries for free.

Over-the-Top Drinking, Las Vegas–Style

A $3,000 cocktail? A $2,000 martini? A $45,000 magnum of wine? They're all the rage in Las Vegas, the place where extravagance seems to be a way of life. Although it's hard to tell how many people actually buy any of these alcoholic elixirs, listing them on the menu of the city's most exclusive lounges and restaurants has become de rigueur.

Ounce for ounce, the most expensive mixed drink in the city may be the MGM Grand's Ménage à Trois, a sinful concoction of Cristal Rosé, Hennessy Ellipse, and Grand Marnier Cent-cinquantenaire that is decorated with 23-karat gold flakes and liquid gold syrup and includes a gold straw studded with a nine-point diamond. Available in the Tryst nightclub, the cocktail costs $3,000, but you can keep the straw.

At Body English, a club at the Hard Rock Hotel and Casino, those with the cash can indulge in the $2,000 Presidential Martini. According to the *Las Vegas Advisor* newsletter, the martini is a mixture of Rémy Martin Louis XIII cognac, 150-year-old Grand Marnier, and a splash of Dom Perignon champagne. It also comes with a keepsake: a ruby-and-diamond-encrusted swizzle stick, which you can take home.

Las Vegas offers plenty of vintage wines that cost thousands of dollars per bottle, but perhaps the priciest is a $45,000 magnum of 1900 Chateau Petrus, available at Fleur de Lys at the Mandalay Bay.

Compared to those, the $99 Goddess Elixir Margarita at the Isla Mexican Kitchen and Tequila Bar at Treasure Island is a regular bargain. There, the "Tequila Goddess," a 6-foot-tall blond, prepares margaritas tableside. The Goddess Elixir is made from five-year-aged Herradura Selección Suprema tequila, Grand Marnier 100-Year Anniversary, Cointreau, and fresh citrus juices.

Bottoms up!

Since hamburger is essentially chopped-up steak, it should come as no surprise that Las Vegas also offers some of the world's most expensive steaks. For instance, at the Bradley Odgen restaurant in Caesars Palace in Las Vegas, the "triple-seared" Japanese Kobe steak runs about $33 an ounce, or about $264 for an eight-ounce cut. ForbesTraveler.com reports that Kobe beef, called "Wagyu" in Japan, has a pale, marbled appearance and "comes from cattle that, according to legend, are fed beer and massaged by human hands."

Say "I Do" and Hold the Fries

The concept of a "quickie" marriage in Las Vegas takes on new meaning when the vows are exchanged at a drive-through wedding chapel. A handful of wedding chapels offer mobile nuptials—the bride and groom drive up to a window or enclosure, pay their money, exchange vows and rings before a minister, sign a few papers, and hit the road.

Charolette Richards, owner of the Little White Wedding Chapel, is credited with inventing the Las Vegas drive-through wedding in the early 1990s. Richards said she came up with the idea after watching a handicapped couple struggle with getting out of their car. She asked her son, a contractor, to knock out a wall and build a drive-up window. After the new nuptial stage opened, it was such a hit that it began attracting all kinds of couples, as well as imitators. Now, at least two other chapels offer similar drive-through weddings.

Richards's "fast-food"-style wedding operation is known as the Tunnel of Love. Open 24/7, the Tunnel of Love (1301 Las Vegas Boulevard South) incorporates a long overhead canopy painted with stars and cupidlike cherubs (Richards has expanded the original drive-up window). The basic wedding cost about $40 and takes only fifteen minutes. At the Garden of Love (1431 Las Vegas Boulevard South), the drive-through window is little more than a bank-teller-type window. You drive up, you pay your money, the minister appears in the window, and you tie the knot. Over at A Special Memory Wedding

The fast food of lifetime commitments—the drive-up wedding window at the Little White Wedding Chapel.

Chapel (800 South Fourth Street), the drive-up window is easy to spot: It has a large neon DRIVE UP sign and, like the others, is open all the time. The basic in-and-out wedding is $25, plus minister gratuity ($40 recommended), which includes wedding music and the ceremony.

For a price all of the drive-through wedding chapels offer additional amenities, such as supplying the betrothed with a stretch limo, a Hummer, or a pink Cadillac for the drive-through or having the ceremony performed by an Elvis impersonator.

Viva Las Weddings

On May 1, 1967, rock 'n' roll icon Elvis Presley married Priscilla Beaulieu in an eight-minute ceremony at the original Aladdin Hotel in Las Vegas. That unique combination of Elvis and Las Vegas weddings proved to be an unbeatable union years later when the Graceland Wedding Chapel started offering Elvis-themed nuptials, complete with an Elvis impersonator who entertained during the event. The concept was a smash, and these days Elvis ceremonies are available at nearly half a dozen Las Vegas wedding chapels.

The Graceland Wedding Chapel offers a variety of Elvis wedding packages that can include having Elvis walk the bride down the aisle, give her away, and provide musical accompaniment. The number of songs depends on the package. Graceland's Elvis, however, prefers not to perform actual weddings, although he will renew wedding vows. Of special note is the "Dueling Elvis" package, which, for $799, offers two different Elvis impersonators representing two different stages in his career (the gold-lamé, youthful Elvis versus the sequined-jumpsuit, 1970s Elvis).

At the appropriately named Viva Las Vegas Chapel, the Elvis/Blue Hawaii package includes use of the Elvis Chapel, which is covered with Elvis memorabilia, as well as an Elvis minister, a tropical setting, and a hula girl dancing to the "Hawaiian Wedding Song" (or you can substitute a Priscilla impersonator as the matron of honor)—all for about $700. The Garden of Love wedding chapel has Elvis packages that range from $249 to $499 and include songs by an Elvis impersonator, limo service, flowers, photos, and, with the purchase of the deluxe package, a keepsake CD by the Elvis impersonator.

Rolling Lucky 7s on Your Wedding Day

On July 7, 2007, thousands of couples flocked to Las Vegas to exchange wedding vows. The occasion was the opportunity to marry on 7-7-7, a date considered lucky by many. In the casino industry, three 7s on a slot machine means a winner, and seven can be a winning number in the game of craps. Moreover, according to the Book of Genesis, God created the world in seven days. The Clark County Marriage License Bureau in Las Vegas estimated that the number of people married on 7-7-7 was about ten times more than the average.

Of course, never let it be said that Las Vegas doesn't know how to turn something to its advantage. A free mass wedding ceremony was available (with more customized packages available for $77.77) at the Texas Station, while couples could tie the knot at the Mandalay Bay with floral leis, a champagne toast, a buffet dinner, and entertainment by KC and the Sunshine Band for only $1,777. The Flamingo hosted seventy-seven different weddings at seven outdoor sites, and seven lucky couples who married at Paris Las Vegas received certificates to celebrate their one-year anniversary with a night's stay at the hotel and a fancy $777 meal. The Ritz-Carlton offered the toniest wedding package, called the "Seven Ways of Wonderment," which included two nights in a seventh-floor room, a seven-course meal, seven hours of spa treatments, and a shopping voucher worth $777 at Neiman-Marcus for $7,707.

There was no mention, however, of a money-back guarantee.

Will It Play in . . . Las Vegas?

Years ago, the question "Will it play in Peoria?" was traditionally asked because that central Illinois city was thought to best represent typical, average, mainstream America. Consumer companies, movie studios, recording firms, and television networks often viewed Peoria as a bellwether for the country—if something worked in Peoria, it would work anywhere in the United States. In the 1960s and 1970s, Peoria was a frequent test market for new products, albums, political initiatives, films, and TV shows.

Move over, Peoria. In 2001 CBS Television City, a research center for testing new TV shows, opened inside the MGM Grand Hotel in Las Vegas. "Drawing on a Las Vegas tourist base of thirty-seven million annual visitors will give us a significant competitive advantage as we develop the programming of the future," said Leslie Moonves, president and chief executive officer of CBS Television.

The state-of-the-art facility screens pilots and shows in production for test audiences. Participants will view not only potential CBS shows but also programs by other networks owned by Viacom, including MTV, VH1, Nickelodeon, Showtime, TNN, CW, and CMT.

CBS Television City has two screening rooms, each of which seats twenty-five and is equipped with ACNielsen's ReelResearch testing system. Every seat has a touch-screen computer linked to the Internet, which allows CBS or the other networks in New York and Los Angeles to interact with the audience. The center also has two focus-group rooms with videoconferencing capabilities and a promotional display with forty-six video screens, a 3-foot-by-3-foot video cube, a video wall, and a digital projection wall.

Best of all—it's easy and free. To participate, pick up a ticket as you enter the MGM from the parking garage or in front of the research center. Register at the counter in front of the center and line up about ten minutes before the scheduled time. A few minutes before the screening starts, you file into one of the screening rooms, find a seat, listen to the instructions on how to use the equipment,

The CBS TV City, tucked inside the MGM Grand Hotel, offers tourists a chance to be a guinea pig for new TV shows.

and then enjoy the show. After you view the program, which can last from thirty minutes to an hour, the survey portion of your visit lasts about fifteen minutes. An estimated four hundred to five hundred people pass through the testing center each day.

CBS recently added seventy-five solo, 19-inch, touch-screen kiosks that allow people to view programs outside of the group setting. Viewers can join in more individualized research sessions by viewing content from the kiosk and reacting to the programming by answering survey questions on the kiosk.

CBS Television City is located at 3799 South Las Vegas Boulevard, inside the MGM Grand Hotel. Hours are 10:00 a.m. to 9:00 p.m. Children must be at least ten years old and accompanied by an adult. Of course, in order to exit, you must pass through the obligatory gift shop. It is filled with CBS- and Viacom-related merchandise, including logo T-shirts, hats, toys, and computer games based on popular shows.

They certainly don't have anything like this in Peoria.

The World's Most Powerful Flashlight

The bright beacon atop the pyramid-shaped Luxor in Las Vegas, which shines directly upward into the sky, is the world's strongest beam of light. Though appearing to be a single beam, the light is actually produced by 39 individual xenon lamps (each of which costs about $1,200), which together generate 315,000 watts of illumination, or about 40 billion candlepower. The lamps, which burn for about 2,000 hours, are enhanced by specially designed curved mirrors, which, according to the Luxor, reflect up to 94 percent of the light from the xenon beams. The mirrors, upgraded in 2000, allow

Photo courtesy of Luxor Hotel

ET semaphore home! As bright as 40 billion candles, the light at the top of the Luxor can be seen from outer space.

fewer lamps to produce more candlepower and cut the cost of turning it on by more than half.

The Luxor's light is said to be visible from space, although that's never been proven. On clear nights the bright beacon can be seen from as far south as Laughlin and as far north as Mesquite. That intense brightness has an unintended side effect: In most years the light attracts millions of moths, which swarm the top of the black-glass Luxor pyramid. Nevada agriculturalist Shirlene Wayland notes that wet years create ideal breeding conditions for the moths, which hatch in the spring. The ultraviolet, short wavelength of the beam is irresistible to the bugs. She says that they don't pose a health risk and generally disappear when the weather warms up.

The Luxor boasts one of the world's largest atriums—it is 30 stories high (350 feet) and encompasses 29 million cubic feet, or big enough to hold nine 747 Boeing airplanes. The hotel's unusual triangular design required some creative thinking when it came to such things as elevators. As a result, Luxor has "inclinators," which travel along the inner walls of the pyramid at a 39-degree angle.

When it opened in 1993, the Luxor had an interior river—called the Nile River, naturally—that encircled the atrium and carried guests to the inclinators from the hotel lobby. The river was removed a couple of years later after guests complained that it took too long to get to their rooms. According to others, however, the river was taken out because too many people had reported seeing the ghosts of three construction workers who had died during the hotel's construction.

The Other City of Light

In the 1990s Las Vegas discovered the world. That's when elaborate megaresorts with geographic themes became the rage. Within a few short years, visitors could find the Ancient Egyptian–influenced Luxor, with a hotel shaped like a pyramid; the Italian Venetian, which has its own canals; New York New York, with its miniature Empire State Building and Statue of Liberty; and Paris Las Vegas. The latter opened in 1999 and incorporates many familiar French landmarks and images, including a huge sign in the shape of a Montgolfier balloon, a two-thirds-size Arc de Triomphe, and a nearly half-scale replica of the Eiffel Tower.

This 50-story faux Eiffel Tower is a nearly exact reproduction of the original, right down to the glass elevators and large rivet beams. The 5,000-ton welded-steel tower rises 540 feet above the ground (the original is 1,063 feet high) and offers sweet views of the entire city from an observation deck at the top. A gourmet restaurant on the eleventh floor also offers panoramic views.

Paris Las Vegas's Eiffel Tower is the largest reproduction of the tower in the world (around the world there are about eighteen replicas, ranging in size from 540 feet to 10 feet). According to some reports, when the tower was originally proposed, it was to be a full-size replica but was reduced in size because the property was too close to the Las Vegas McCarran International Airport.

Paris Las Vegas (3655 Las Vegas Boulevard South) has had a convoluted history. The resort, which cost about $785 million, was originally proposed by Bally's, but it became part of Hilton Hotels in 1996 when Hilton purchased Bally's. In 2000 Hilton merged with Caesars Entertainment and then, in 2004, became part of Harrah's. According to some sources, when Hilton began construction of the project, it was originally going to be called Paris Hilton, after the granddaughter of company owner Barron Hilton.

Like the real one, the Paris Las Vegas Eiffel Tower is open to the public. Cost is $9 for adults, $7 for seniors and children six to twelve, and free for those five and under. Between 9:30 a.m. and 12:30 a.m., weather permitting, visitors can ride an elevator to the observation deck near the top of the monolith. As you ascend, a knowledgeable elevator attendant explains the history of the original Eiffel Tower and points out various Las Vegas landmarks. The observation platform, which is 460 feet above the ground, offers spectacular views of the Las Vegas Strip and the entire Las Vegas Valley.

Photo courtesy of Paris Las Vegas

The faux Eiffel Tower at Paris Las Vegas allows you to experience virtual French attractions.

For a half-buck, you can also use one of several strategically placed telescopes that offer even better views. The deck is one of the best places to watch the Bellagio's famed water fountain show (directly west).

For a one-of-a-kind dining experience, the Eiffel Tower Restaurant offers gourmet French cuisine, including dishes such as cold smoked salmon, blue-cheese soufflé pudding, roasted foie gras, escargots, and sautéed Casco Bay sea scallops. The restaurant is open daily for lunch from 11:00 a.m. to 3:30 p.m. and for dinner from 5:00 to 10:00 p.m. Advance reservations are required.

Bon appétit.

Ode to Liberace

During the 1950s and 1960s, the original king of bling was pianist Liberace, who pioneered the use of outrageous outfits, extravagant jewelry, and over-the-top stage shows long before Elton John learned to read music. He was born Wladziu Valentino Liberace in 1919, and his musical skills were recognized early. He performed with the Chicago Symphony at age fourteen and in 1944 made his first Las Vegas appearance at the Last Frontier.

During the 1950s Liberace hosted a popular national television program, appeared in several movies, and became the highest-paid performer in Las Vegas. In 1976 he founded the nonprofit Liberace Foundation for the Performing and Creative Arts, which provides music scholarships to colleges throughout the country. The Liberace Museum opened in 1979 and serves as the key funding arm for the foundation.

Although Liberace has been dead since 1987, you wouldn't know it from the size of the crowds still flocking to the Las Vegas museum that bears his name. People are reverential—almost as though they're viewing the Sistine Chapel—as they file by large, glass display cases filled with the bejeweled and feathered costumes and capes favored by the pianist who dubbed himself "Mr. Showmanship."

The museum is divided into three main exhibit areas in two locations in a shopping center that was owned by Liberace. The main building contains the entertainer's collections of cars and pianos, while the annex houses his extravagant outfits and jewelry as well as a re-creation of his Palm Springs bedroom and office. The latter includes a massive inlaid and ormolued Louis XV desk, which once belonged to Czar Nicholas II of Russia. Adjacent is the library, which has Liberace's collection of miniature pianos, family photos, letters from friends, and sheet music.

During his life Liberace acquired more than forty vintage pianos. Eighteen of the best are displayed, including Chopin's French Pleyel, built in the early 1800s; an 1860 Giraffe upright piano with

The Liberace Museum is a shrine to the rhinestones and sequins of the late showman, who died in 1987.

an unusual metal harp-shaped frame; George Gershwin's Chickory Piano; and a 1788 Broadwood Grand Piano. The entertainer also collected cars—he owned more than fifty—and several are exhibited, including a Rolls Royce covered with thousands of mirrors, a 1934 Mercedes Excalibur covered with rhinestones, and a pink Volks Royce, which is a Volkswagen customized to resemble a Rolls.

The costume gallery in the annex displays the clothing most associated with Liberace, such as a 125-pound, black mink cape covered with rhinestones (valued at $750,000) and hot pants decorated with red, white, and blue rhinestones, which the entertainer wore when he performed in New York for the one hundredth birthday of the

Statue of Liberty. Also on display is Liberace's stage jewelry, including a candelabra ring with platinum candlesticks and diamond flames and a unique piano-shaped ring that contains 260 diamonds set in white and yellow gold.

And, of course, it should come as no surprise that the museum has the world's largest Austrian rhinestone, a gift to Liberace, which has 115,000 carats and weighs more than 50 pounds. The Liberace Museum is located at 1775 East Tropicana Avenue in Las Vegas. Donations to the museum are $12.50 for adults, $8.50 for seniors and students with ID; children under ten are admitted free. The museum is open Tuesday through Saturday from 10:00 a.m. to 5:00 p.m. and Sunday from noon to 4:00 p.m.

The Brain Doctor's Hobby

Like some modern-day version of the mythical town of Brigadoon, which was said to appear for only one day every century, Dr. Lonnie Hammergren opens the doors to his Castillo del Sol (Castle of the Sun) to the curious public just once a year—on October 31, which is Nevada Admission Day. Of course, the reason for the interest in Hammergren's home is that for the past several decades the eccentric Las Vegas brain surgeon and former Nevada lieutenant governor has amassed a large and eclectic collection of oddities—or junk, as some would say—ranging from an exercise bike once owned by Tarzan actor Johnny Weismuller to a life-size replica of a *Camarasaurus* dinosaur skeleton that was constructed in 1937 for a movie.

Over the years Dr. Hammergren has acquired so many thousands of unusual items that his house at 4218 Ridgecrest Drive not only has been expanded to include a second story but also has swallowed up two neighboring homes. The result is a bizarre, sprawling compound that has an observatory and planetarium, more than a dozen rooms jammed with items, and a backyard that is a topographical representation of the state of Nevada.

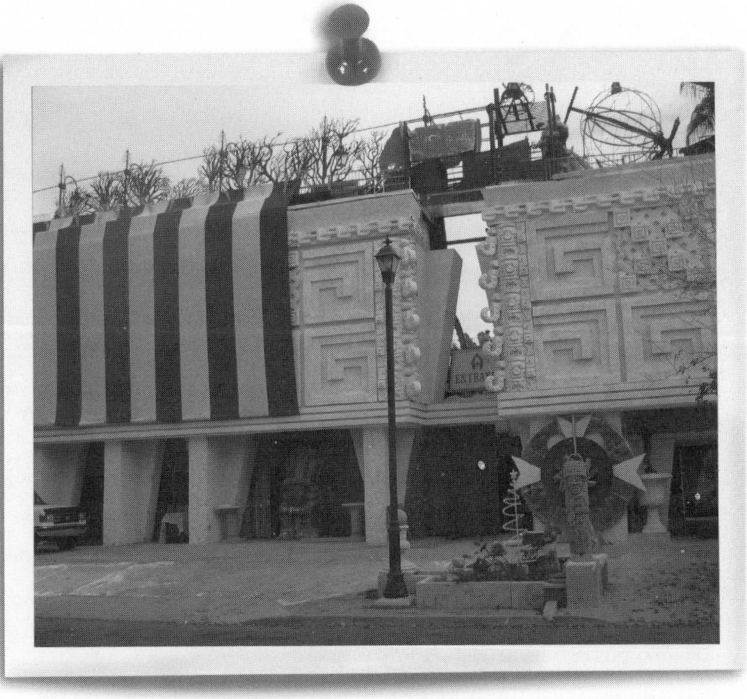

Proving that some folks have more money than taste, Dr. Lonnie Hammergren's funhouse threatens to overwhelm its suburban neighbors.

Castillo del Sol is located in the middle of a residential neighborhood, and it's easy to spot from the street—the front of the house resembles a Mayan temple (it's based on the Palace of the Governor in the Mayan ruins of Uxmal in the Yucatán), a giant replica of the Statue of Liberty's hand and torch peeks up from the backyard, and a doppelgänger of Stonehenge sits on the roof. Dr. Hammergren bought the original house, a four-bedroom, wood-frame and stucco model, in 1972 for $45,000. He began collecting retired neon signs, giant movie props, and other paraphernalia, which soon filled his backyard. To accommodate his growing menagerie, he bought connecting homes, eventually creating a two-acre, 12,500-square-foot complex devoted to his insatiable appetite for the strange and unusual.

Inside, the home is divided into several themed rooms. For example, the Music Room has Liberace's honky-tonk piano and other musical instruments, each with a story. A Toy Room, a car collection, and an Egyptian tomb are other highlights. The backyard—voted "Worst Las Vegas Eyesore" in 1997 by readers of the *Las Vegas Review-Journal*—is a hodgepodge of stuff, including an Apollo training capsule, a replica of a space shuttle, a submarine from the TV show *Voyage to the Bottom of the Sea,* a narrow-gauge mining railroad, a Batmobile, a model of the Parthenon, and a giant scale model of Hoover Dam, built for the doctor by workmen who constructed the dam in 1935. He also owns the doors to the first Clark County jail; an observatory and a planetarium; a massive, fire-breathing dragon that was once used in a casino show; a former brothel building (now used for storage); and a replica of the Lincoln Monument.

And he's not done. In 2006 Dr. Hammergren held a yard sale to get rid of some of the stuff that even he thinks is junk. The purpose of the sale wasn't to begin trimming his massive collection. Rather, he needed to make room for a new acquisition—he had just purchased the roller coaster that had been removed from the top of the Stratosphere Tower.

Where to Find Vegas's Mob Roots

The public's appetite for gangsters is seemingly insatiable—particularly when it comes to Las Vegas. Not surprisingly, a local tour operator has created the Vegas Mob Tour, a two-and-a-half-hour bus excursion through the city to the locations associated with some of the most infamous of these legendary "wiseguys."

Founder Robert Allen, a local musician, comic, and tour promoter, says the tour is based on stories described in the book *The Battle for Las Vegas* by Dennis Griffin as well as interviews with retired FBI agent Dennis Arnoldy and former mob enforcer Frank Cullota. The tour begins with a short film about Las Vegas's mob past and continues to the locations of some of the more infamous mob-related

Gangster Benjamin "Bugsy" Siegel briefly owned a piece of the El Cortez Hotel in downtown Las Vegas.

activities, including crime and murder scenes. To enhance the experience, tour guides dress in pin-striped suits and fedoras.

The Vegas Mob Tour is offered Saturday through Thursday at 9:30 p.m. The tour starts at the Greek Isles Hotel & Casino (305 Convention Center Drive) and is open to anyone sixteen or older. Tickets are $56.25 per person. For information call (702) 737-5540.

Of course, it's not necessary to take a tour to visit places associated with some of the city's most infamous figures. In 2006 the *Las Vegas Review-Journal*'s Corey Levitan concocted a self-guided "Wise Guide" to mobster tour stops, including the following:

- El Cortez Hotel (600 Fremont Street), once owned by Benjamin "Bugsy" Siegel. He and his partners assumed control of the property in 1943. When Siegel sold his share, he used the profits to finance the construction of the Flamingo, the first luxury hotel on the Las Vegas Strip.

Haunted Las Vegas

Robert Allen, founder of the Vegas Mob Tour, has a thing for colorful Las Vegas history. He has also created the Haunted Vegas Tour, a two-and-a-half-hour night-time motor coach journey to Las Vegas locales inhabited, it is said, by restless spirits. As with the Mob Tour, Allen has based the ghost tour on a book, in this case Jane Oberding's *Haunted Nevada*, and consulted with a paranormal historian, Tim Cridland.

The Haunted Vegas Tour begins with a half-hour comedy show that serves as a warm-up for the more serious bus trip. The tour passes by more than a dozen places where alleged paranormal activity has occurred, including the former home of entertainer Redd Foxx at 5460 South Eastern Avenue (now a realty office), which is said to be haunted by his ghost; backstage at the Las Vegas Hilton, where a spectral Elvis has been sighted; and the spot on Flamingo and Koval Roads where rapper Tupac Shakur was shot and killed and where his spirit has been seen. The tour also passes the Flamingo, where "Bugsy" Siegel's ghost is said to still roam, and Carlucci's Tivoli Gardens restaurant, where Liberace reportedly makes appearances (he once owned it), and makes a brief stop at Fox Ridge Park in Henderson, where the ghost of a little boy occasionally makes an empty playground swing begin to move. Tours are offered Friday through Monday at 9:00 p.m. at the Greek Isles Hotel. Cost is $48.25 per person. For more information, go to www.hauntedvegastours.com.

The ghost of entertainer Redd Foxx is said to haunt his former South Las Vegas home, now a realty office.

- Spilotro Headquarters (former site of Gold Rush Jewelers, at 228 West Sahara Avenue), the main office of mob enforcer Tony Spilotro. He is reputed to have killed nearly two dozen people across the country in the 1970s and 1980s. Joe Pesci played a character based on Spilotro in the 1995 film *Casino*. Spilotro used the store, which wasn't listed in the Yellow Pages, to fence stolen wares.
- Meadows Casino (former site at Twenty-fifth Street and Boulder Highway). When it opened in 1931, the Meadows was the first legal gambling casino in Las Vegas. It was built by mobster Tony Cornero, a bootlegger and operator of gambling ships off the coast of southern California.
- Flamingo Hotel (3555 Las Vegas Boulevard South), site of the first true gambling resort in Las Vegas. "Bugsy" Siegel built the Flamingo in 1946. Although nothing remains of the original buildings, there are rumors that his ghost can be seen strolling through the rose garden built on the site of his former suite.
- Murder site (Heritage Square Townhouses, 3655 Mount Vernon Avenue). On January 6, 1997, in this modest apartment complex, "Fat Herbie" Blitzstein, a former member of Tony Spilotro's inner circle, was gunned down in his home.

The World's Most Famous Wipeout

When legendary daredevil Robert "Evel" Knievel died in 2007, nearly every televised news report included footage of one of his most *famous* stunts—his attempt on December 31, 1967, to leap over the fountains in front of Caesars Palace in Las Vegas on his motorcycle. At the time, Knievel was the world's most famous stuntman. He was a regular on network TV talk shows and had gained fame for having piloted a bike over sixteen cars.

The Caesars Palace jump attracted thousands of spectators, interested in seeing whether he could clear the 151 feet of water fountains. The ride began well, but, Knievel later recalled, just as he hit the takeoff ramp, he felt the motorcycle suddenly decelerate. The

The site of one of the world's most famous crashes: In 1967 Evel Knievel cleared the fountains in front of Caesars Palace but crashed upon landing.

loss of power on the takeoff caused his bike to come up short on the landing. He easily cleared the fountains but landed awkwardly on the lip of a safety ramp supported by a van. Video footage shows the handlebars being ripped from his hands as he flipped over them and painfully skidded and bounced for several dozen yards on hard pavement before finally coming to a stop. The accident resulted in a shattered pelvis and right femur, a fractured hip, broken ankles and wrist, and a severe concussion and left him in a coma for twenty-nine days. To rebuild his leg, doctors had to insert a 2-foot-long, 3-inch-wide strip of steel.

Ironically, not completing the jump made Knievel more famous than before. The nation closely watched his recovery, and ABC bought the rights to the film of his jump (he had personally paid to film the jump because none of the networks were interested in covering it). Told by his doctors that he not only would never jump again but probably would not walk without a cane, Knievel decided to jump over fifteen cars just five months after this near-fatal crash at Caesars. He also failed to nail this jump and broke his right leg and foot. In April 1989 Knievel's son, Robbie, also a stunt rider, returned to the site of his father's most famous crash and successfully jumped over the Caesars Palace fountains.

Even though many of Evel Knievel's jumping records have been surpassed since he retired in 1981, he has earned a spot in the *Guinness Book of World Records*—for most broken bones.

Lions, Lions, Lions (Not Lying)

With 5,044 rooms, the MGM Grand in Las Vegas is the biggest hotel in North America. Everything about the resort is bigger than life. It has the largest casino in Las Vegas, with 171,500 square feet of tables and games, as well as 16 restaurants; 7 outdoor pools, rivers, and waterfalls that cover 6.6 acres; and a 380,000-square-foot convention center. And it has the largest bronze statue of an animal in the United States. Perched on a 25-foot pedestal over the entrance to the megaresort is a 45-foot-tall, gold-colored lion named Leo. The statue weighs nearly 100,000 pounds and was cast in 1,600 individual, half-inch-thick bronze plates and welded together over a steel skeleton.

Leo is actually the second lion to grace the hotel entrance. When the resort opened in 1993, its front entry was built in the shape of a large, stylized lion's head. Guests entered the building through the mouth of the lion. Unfortunately, according to several sources, shortly after the hotel opened, management learned that walking into a lion's mouth was considered bad luck in many cultures. A few years

Photo courtesy of MGM Grand Mirage

The MGM Grand Hotel's exotic lion habitat is home of its own pride of the majestic felines.

later, the entrance was remodeled to remove the lion's-mouth entry. The statue of Leo, the longtime corporate symbol for MGM Grand, was erected in 1997.

In keeping with the lion theme, in 1999 the MGM Grand constructed the MGM Lion Habitat, a lion exhibit inside the hotel-casino. The habitat, a free attraction, stands three stories high, with giant 1.5-inch-thick Plexiglas walls on three sides that afford views of the animals. A see-through Plexiglas tunnel passes through the enclosure and offers close-up looks at the lions. Keith Evans, an exotic feline trainer and conservationist, manages the habitat and owns the animals, which live on an eight-and-a-half-acre ranch located about 12 miles from the hotel. The lions are rotated daily through the exhibit and are allowed to remain for a maximum of only six hours; they then spend at least two days off at the ranch.

The habitat incorporates a faux jungle theme with a pool, shade trees, and large boulders. Because large cats spend eighteen to twenty hours a day sleeping, they usually aren't very active. Occasionally, though, visitors arrive just as one is getting bathed, playing, grooming, or feeding. Periodically, trainers make presentations and explain the animals' habits and behavior. The habitat is open daily from 11:00 a.m. to 10:00 p.m.

World's Largest Simultaneous Toast and One Big Cake

The distinction for the world's biggest toast goes—not surprisingly—to the city of Las Vegas and Las Vegas and Beaulieu Vineyard, which jointly sponsored a massive ceremony on December 31, 2005, as part of Las Vegas's centennial celebration. A record 13,500 participants stood under the canopy of the Fremont Street Experience, simultaneously raised their glasses in unison, and drank. The event involved more than sixty staff and volunteers, who greeted and registered the participants, checked identification, and poured more than 200 cases of a special "Century Cellars" Chardonnay made by Beaulieu Vineyards. The record shattered the previous winner, a simultaneous toast by 10,079 folks held by a Japanese sake company.

Las Vegas mayor Oscar Goodman noted that "Las Vegas knows how to throw a party, and this confirms that we do it bigger and better than anyone."

Also during the yearlong Las Vegas centennial celebration, the city set the record for the world's largest birthday cake. The 130,000-pound buttercream yellow cake was the result of a combined effort by the Las Vegas Centennial Committee, Sara Lee Corporation, and more than 1,000 volunteers.

The actual cake was baked at Sara Lee's facility in North Carolina and driven to Las Vegas in 8 refrigerated semis. The preparation and baking took more than 14 hours and involved 24,000 pounds of flour, 18,000 pounds of sugar, and 130,000 eggs. Sara Lee executive chef Brian Averna flew from Connecticut to oversee the assembling of the 102-foot-long cake, which consisted of 30,240 half-sheet panels covered by nearly 40,000 pounds of frosting. The Vegas Centennial cake surpassed the previous world record cake of 128,360 pounds, set in Fort Wayne, Alabama.

According to the *Guinness Book of World Records* rules, the cake must contain traditional ingredients in the correct proportions, must be prepared in the same manner as a normal-size cake, must be prepared to appropriate hygiene standards, must be completely edible and safe to consume, and must be iced over so that no joint can be seen between the various cake sheets.

A Place Where High Rollers Can Hoop It Up

In recent years the Palms Hotel-Casino has become one of the hippest places in Las Vegas. It's owned and operated by the Maloof family, which also owns the Sacramento Kings professional basketball team. George Maloof Jr. is the president of the 802-room Palms Hotel, which contains a 95,000-square-foot casino, a recording studio, and a 2,200-seat showroom. When the Palms opened in 2001, Maloof quickly positioned it as a Las Vegas hot spot by hosting the 2002 season of the MTV reality show *The Real World* in his hotel as well as two seasons of Bravo's *Celebrity Poker Showdown* and the 2007 MTV Video Music Awards. He also established two nightclubs that cater to sports and entertainment celebrities—Ghostbar and Rain. As an aside, Ghostbar, which is located on the fifty-fifth floor of the Palms, has a Plexiglas cutout on its patio that allows you to look down to street level, a drop of 450 feet.

In addition, the Palms has generated considerable buzz by building some of the most expensive and trendy high-roller suites in town, including the 3,000-square-foot Real World Suite (where the show was filmed), the 5,000-square-foot Kingpin Suite (with two state-of-the-art bowling lanes, a pool table, and a theater-size projection TV for $7,500 to $15,000 a night), and the 1,500-square-foot Erotica Suite (with a stripper pole, private show shower, and rotating bed).

Reflecting the family's ownership of a National Basketball Association (NBA) franchise, the 10,000-square-foot NBA-themed Hardwood Suite is the ultimate crib for the hard-core basketball fan. It's a two-level party room that includes an indoor basketball half court, locker room, scoreboard, pool table, poker table, and dance floor. The suite also has three NBA-size Murphy beds, a dining area, a ten-person Jacuzzi tub, and a living room with 42-inch plasma-screen TVs. According to *USA Today,* guests can also hire a cheerleader ($750 for four hours) and a referee ($250). The cost of the room is said to be $25,000 per night, although few actually pay that much because these suites are generally provided at no charge to the "whales," a term for gamblers with a minimum $1 million line of credit with the casino.

The Hugh Hefner Sky Villa opened in 2006 in conjunction with the opening of a new Playboy Club in the Palms. The Palms Playboy Club revived a legendary but defunct nightclub franchise that had folded in 1991. The original clubs, which once operated in cities throughout the world, were associated with the *Playboy* men's magazine, founded by Hugh Hefner. The Hefner Sky Villa is a 9,000-square-foot suite inspired by Hefner's living quarters in the famed Playboy Mansion in

Los Angeles. Located on the thirty-fourth and thirty-fifth floors of the Palms' Fantasy Tower, the Hefner suite is decorated in red and black with leather wallpaper and marble flooring. In addition to a spectacular view, it includes a rotating bed, a private glass elevator, two bedrooms, a massage room, an eight-person Jacuzzi, a sauna, and a workout room. Original artwork selected by Hefner, including *Playboy* magazine covers and centerfolds, graces the walls. If you're not a whale, the cost is reportedly a cool $40,000 a night—bunnies not included.

The $54 Million Tear

In September 2006, casino magnate Steve Wynn, owner of Wynn Resorts, was showing off his prize Picasso painting *Le Rêve,* which is French for "The Dream." Just a day before, Wynn had completed the sale of the painting of Picasso's mistress to art collector Steven Cohen for a record price of $139 million. While gesturing to his guests—who included journalist Barbara Walters and screenwriters Nora Ephron and Nicholas Pileggi—Wynn, who suffers from retinitis pigmentosa, an eye disease restricting peripheral vision, accidentally struck the painting with his right elbow and tore a hole the size of a thumb into the canvas. When it happened, Ephron said that Wynn's response was, "Oh, s**t, look what I've done. Thank goodness it was me."

The tear may have decreased the painting's value by a whopping $54 million.

As a result of the mishap, Wynn withdrew the painting from the sale and announced plans to restore and keep it. He has estimated that it will cost about $85,000 to restore the famous painting. Once the canvas is repaired, art experts say the tear will not be visible. Had it been sold to Cohen, the price tag would have been the most ever paid for a single piece of art, surpassing the previous record of $135 million paid by cosmetics giant Ronald Lauder in July 2006 for Gustav Klimt's 1907 portrait, *Adele Bloch-Bauer I.*

Wynn, who called it "the world's clumsiest and goofiest thing to do," later sued his insurers, Lloyd's of London, alleging that the com-

Namesake resort owned by Steve Wynn, home of his renowned art collection, including his torn Picasso.

pany had failed to act quickly on his claim that the value of the painting had dropped by so many millions. In his filing Wynn said that he believes the current value of the painting is only $85 million. He said he hopes to recover the difference between what he was going to sell it for and the present value, and he wanted Lloyd's ordered to provide him with a copy of its appraisal, which would include the post-restoration value of the artwork. The Cubist painting, which Wynn purchased in 1997 for $48.4 million, is said to depict Marie-Thérèse Walter, Pablo Picasso's twenty-two-year-old mistress.

Wynn, one of the world's most successful hotel-casino operators, is generally credited with the resurgence and expansion of the Las Vegas Strip in the 1990s. In addition to his self-named resort in Las Vegas, he owns the 600-room Wynn Macau in southeast China and the 2,034-room Encore, a sister property adjacent to Wynn Las Vegas. Before he sold them in 2000, Wynn built the Mirage, Treasure Island, and Bellagio resorts on the Las Vegas Strip. He owns one of the world's most valuable art collections, including works by Picasso, van Gogh, Gauguin, Matisse, and Cézanne, many of which are displayed at Wynn Las Vegas.

Lions and Tigers and—Dolphins, Oh My?

Back in the late 1980s when casino visionary Steve Wynn was building the Mirage Resort, he decided that his property needed something unusual to give it instant must-see credibility as a tourist attraction. He decided it needed dolphins for panache. So he built a dolphin habitat. He also signed mega-popular animal illusionists Siegfried Fischbacher and Roy Horn to a long-term contract and provided the two entertainers with a place to show off their collection of rare white tigers, lions, and other exotic animals.

The result is the Mirage's Secret Garden and Dolphin Habitat, a kind of fantastical, quasi-aquarium and zoo. Tucked into the resort's lushly landscaped grounds, the Secret Garden and Dolphin Habitat is an amazing indulgence in a place that's made excess an art form. Here, visitors can view an elaborate dolphin habitat, home to a family of Atlantic bottlenose dolphins that live in four pools containing 2.5 million gallons of water. The pools, all connected, incorporate an artificial coral reef system and sandy bottoms designed to replicate a

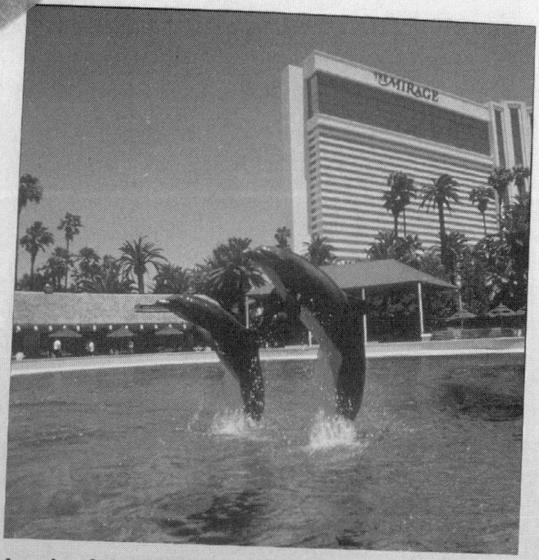

Photo courtesy of the Nevada Commission on Tourism

A pair of dolphins leap through the air at the Mirage Resort's dolphin habitat.

more natural environment. Below the pools is the underwater viewing area, where visitors can see the sleek dolphins swim by windows that look into the center of the pool.

Adjacent to the dolphins is the Secret Garden, a lush, tropical environment that is home to several rare, striped white tigers. The animals' unusual coloration is the result of an uncommon, recessive gene. They were believed to be extinct until a cub was discovered in India in 1951. Siegfried and Roy, who retired from performing a few years ago after Roy was attacked by one of the white tigers during a performance, have devoted considerable energy to preserving the species; they now have nearly two dozen white tigers in their care. The entertainers have also successfully bred and display snow-white tigers (no stripes) as well as a rare snow leopard, white lions, and black panthers. The Secret Garden and Dolphin Habitat (702-791-7188; www.miragehabitat.com) is open 11:00 a.m. to 5:30 p.m. on weekdays and 10:00 a.m. to 5:30 p.m. on weekends.

Catching Big Air

The cool thing about Flyaway Indoor Skydiving, which calls itself America's first vertical wind tunnel, is that you don't have to get into a plane to do it. There's no pilot, no parachute, no worrying about falling to your death. Through the magic of a giant fan in the floor, participants can simulate the experience of skydiving without ever leaving the ground. Thrust from the fan suspends you in the air and provides the closest thing to falling through the sky. You just fly in a column of air about 12 feet across and up to 22 feet high, with vertical airspeeds up to 120 miles per hour.

Flyaway, which attracts about 30,000 skydivers each year, has been simulating skydiving for more than a decade. Participants are given a twenty-minute training class and then suit up in cushioned jumpsuits with goggles, elbow pads, earplugs, and helmets. Usually in groups of five, they file into a round, thickly padded room with a trampoline net floor over the fan with an instructor, who describes what is about to happen and guides them through the process of becoming weightless. The massive fan builds up speed, and suddenly the flyer is virtually weightless. The instructor shows the correct positions for acrobatic maneuvers. Each group has a fifteen-minute session in the tunnel, with each participant getting about three minutes of airtime.

Be aware that the ride is loud. The fan at the base of the tunnel is an actual DC-3 propeller. Flyers are told to relax and learn to fall the right way (to tuck and roll) to avoid injuries. The method basically involves forming your body into a ball when falling. With a bit of practice, flyers can use the bouncy netting to perform somersaults and other stunts. The propeller is usually not set to maximum

Going Weightless in Las Vegas

Decades ago, scientists discovered that by flying an airplane through what is called a parabolic flight maneuver, it was possible to achieve weightlessness without rocketing into outer space. The plane is flown at a high altitude (24,000 feet and above) with a steep climb up, followed by a kind of rolling-over motion. When the plane hits that point where it flies horizontally, passengers experience weightlessness that is identical to being in outer space. Ron Howard utilized the maneuver during the filming of the space scenes in *Apollo 13,* and it was used to create some of the special effects in the *Matrix 2* and *Matrix 3* movies. A Las Vegas company, ZERO-G, offers a similarly lightweight experience to anyone with $3,500 and a strong stomach. Flying out of Las Vegas's McCarran Airport, ZERO-G has already taken more than 3,000 people on its faux-zero-gravity plane rides, including physicist Stephen Hawking, who is almost completely paralyzed; astronaut Buzz Aldrin; designer Martha Stewart; and magician Teller (of Penn and Teller fame).

strength for beginners because it takes time to get the hang of flying.

A new variation on skydiving, including the indoor variety, is skysurfing. This sport involves strapping a board, similar to a snowboard, to your feet and literally surfing through the air during a skydive. Wannabe skysurfers have discovered that Flyaway is a good place to learn how to skysurf before actually jumping out of a plane to try it.

The cost for a session is $70 for a first flight; $35 for a repeat flight on the same day. Hours are 10:00 a.m. to 10:00 p.m. Children under eighteen must be accompanied by a parent. There are weight limits: Men taller than 6 feet can't weigh more than 230 pounds; men shorter than 6 feet can't weigh more than 220 pounds; women taller than 6

You will believe you can fly at the Flyaway Skydiving facility.

feet can't weigh more than 200 pounds; women between 5 feet 6 inches and 6 feet tall can't weigh more than 180 pounds; and women shorter than 5 feet 6 inches can't weigh more than 160 pounds. Flyaway Indoor Skydiving is located at 200 Convention Center Drive in Las Vegas.

Trivia

The Black Book

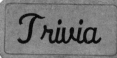

In the 1950s Nevada's image was taking a beating. The crime-fighting Kefauver Committee (named after its chair, Senator Estes Kefauver) had shone a spotlight on Las Vegas's casinos and their relationship to organized crime figures. Congress was considering a 10 percent tax on all gambling, which many politicians regarded as an immoral and corrupting influence. Nevada officials felt pressured to do something, so they created the Nevada Gaming Commission to license casino owners and, later, the Gaming Control Board, to determine owner suitability.

To keep track of the worst gambling cheats and the most "mobbed-up" individuals, in 1960 the Gaming Control Board created "A List of Excluded Persons," or the Black Book (it originally had a black cover), which identified eleven individuals, most with mob backgrounds, who were banned for life from setting foot in any Nevada casino. The original list included Marshall Caifano, an extortionist and top lieutenant in the Chicago crime syndicate; Louis Tom Dragna, head of a southern California organized crime family; Chicago mob boss Sam Giancana; and John Louis Battaglia, a mob hitman who once worked for Al Capone.

Since then, more than fifty individuals have made the list. In fact, the only way off the list is to die. At present, thirty-four men and one woman (Sandra Kay Vaccaro, head of a major slot cheat ring) are in the Black Book. Others in the book include Frank "Lefty" Rosenthal, a mob frontman who was featured in the film *Casino,* and racketeer Francis Citro, who appeared at his Black Book hearing in a tuxedo and told members, "I've never been invited to join anything in my life. I just wanted to show the proper respect."

CHAPTER

2

South
Beyond the Neon

"Nature was in her eccentric mood when forming this region, and turned out some strange results from the store-house of time."
—Thompson and West's *History of Nevada* (1881)

Not all of *southern Nevada's weird stuff is restricted to Las Vegas (although it might seem that way). If you step out of the city's oversize shadow, you'll encounter a number of places and people that are marvelously strange, peculiar, notorious, or just plain interesting. These outlands include natural sites unlike anything else found in the state, such as the bizarre, blood-red rock formations of the Valley of Fire and the multicolored, layer-cake cliffs of the Spring Mountains, as well as man-made spectacles like Hoover Dam, where it's impossible to avoid vertigo if you look over the edge. Some of these places are actually older than Las Vegas, and one of them, Searchlight, was once the largest town in the region. (Searchlight is also the former hometown of 1920s movie stars Clara ["It Girl"] Bow and Rex Bell as well as Oscar-winning costume designer Edith Head.) One former town, St. Thomas, peeks out from beneath the waters of Lake Mead only during drought years, while another, Boulder City, doesn't even allow gambling—which, in southern Nevada, is rarer than finding a casino without a buffet.*

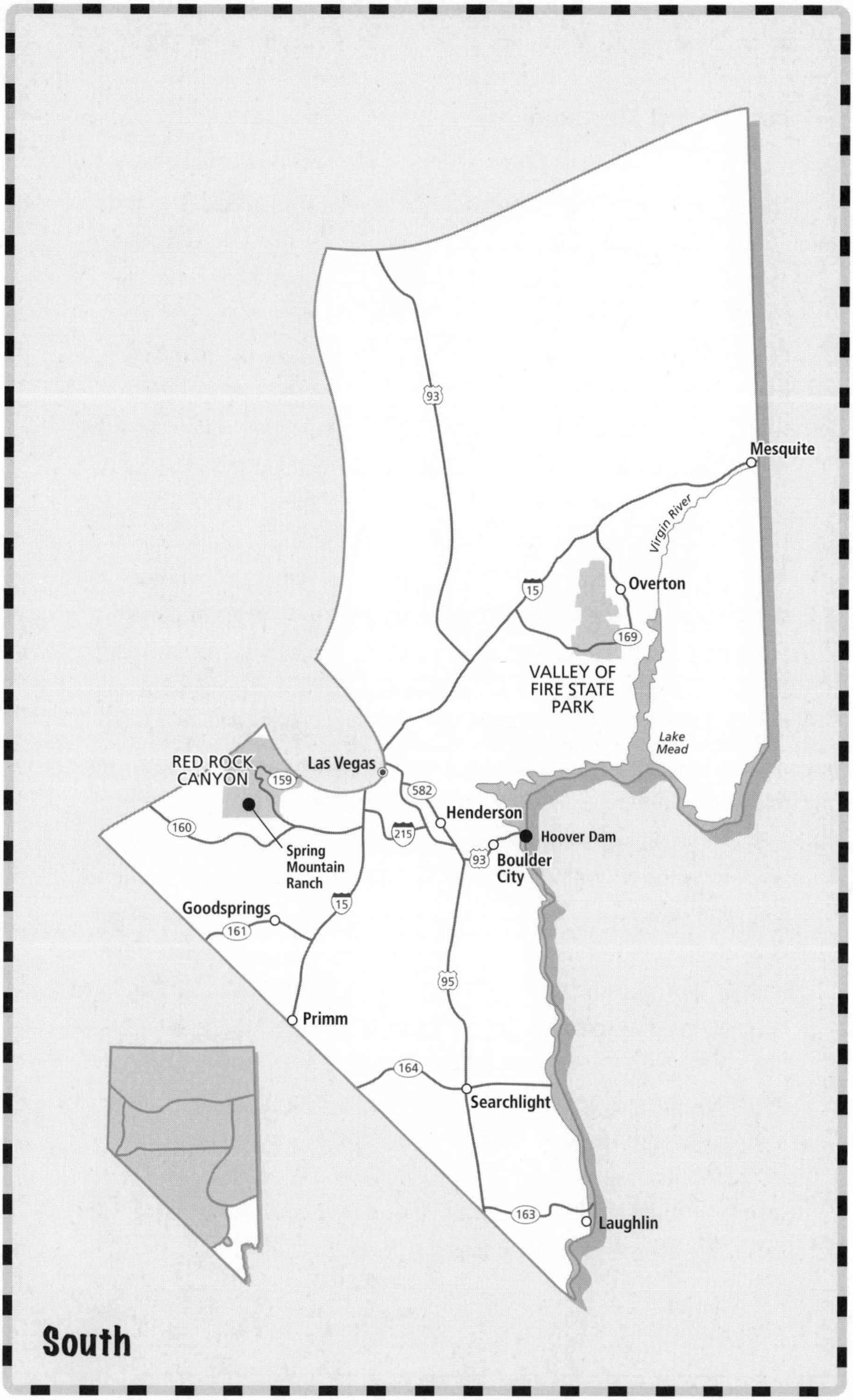

Mesquite
Virgin River
Overton
93
15
169
VALLEY OF
FIRE STATE
PARK
Lake
Mead
RED ROCK
CANYON
Las Vegas
159
582
Henderson
Hoover Dam
160
215
93
Boulder
City
Spring
Mountain
Ranch
Goodsprings
15
161
95
Primm
164
Searchlight
163
Laughlin
South

Boris Karloff Slept Here

Boulder City

The Boulder Dam Hotel, located in the hamlet of Boulder City, about 25 miles southeast of Las Vegas, began life as a glamorous retreat for the rich and famous eager to see Hoover Dam and enjoy the water sports and fishing on Lake Mead. Opened in 1933, it was the most elegant lodging house in southern Nevada, with a wood-paneled lobby and thirty-three air-conditioned guest rooms, each with private, tiled bathrooms. Unlike the rest of the buildings in Boulder City, which had incorporated Art Deco design, owners Raymond Spilsbury and Paul S. "Jimmy" Webb, who had made their money building homes and other real estate projects in southern California, built the two-story hotel in a Dutch colonial style. During its first few years, the hotel was a hit, hosting dignitaries such as the maharaja and maharani of Indore, India; industrialist Cornelius Vanderbilt Jr., who spent part of his honeymoon in the hotel in 1935; photographer Margaret Bourke-White; humorist Will Rogers; and film stars Ronald Coleman, Bette Davis, Boris Karloff, and Harold Lloyd. The owners were so certain of its success that they soon added another fifteen guest rooms and a large dining room.

Unfortunately, Webb's other business ventures didn't fare quite as well, and he allowed the hotel to languish because he was unable to pay for routine maintenance. In 1941 the federal government closed Hoover Dam because of fears about terrorism during World War II, an action that effectively cut off visitors from seeing the hotel's main attraction. Webb sold his portion of the hotel to Spilsbury, who began improving the property and returning it to profitability. However, in January 1945, Spilsbury disappeared. His body was found in the Colorado River a month later. Despite the fact that his feet were tied together with his own belt and his pockets were filled with rocks, the coroner decided it was a suicide.

Go figure—the Boulder Dam Hotel is near Hoover Dam.

Since then, the little hotel in the center of Boulder City has been through more than a dozen owners and an equal number of bankruptcies. In the early 1990s the hotel, which had been listed on the National Register of Historic Places in 1982, was acquired by the Boulder Dam Hotel Association, a nonprofit historic preservation group, which spent more than $2 million renovating the property. Today, the magnificent landmark (www.boulderdamhotel.com) has reopened as a boutique hotel with twenty-one rooms and a restaurant. The first floor has been converted into small shops selling artwork, crafts, antiques, candles, and jewelry.

Cheech and Chong Meet Rhett Butler

Goodsprings

The Pioneer Saloon in the near-ghost town of Goodsprings (located 8 miles north of Jean, which is about 22 miles west of Las Vegas) is probably the only place in the world where you might hear actor Clark Gable mentioned in the same sentence as 1980s stoner comics Cheech and Chong.

Sporting a Mad Max–meets–the–Old West decor, the Pioneer Saloon is housed in a rust-tinted, pressed-metal structure that is said to be one of the oldest and largest stamped-tin buildings (the metal is stamped to resemble bricks) still standing. It sits amidst the ruins

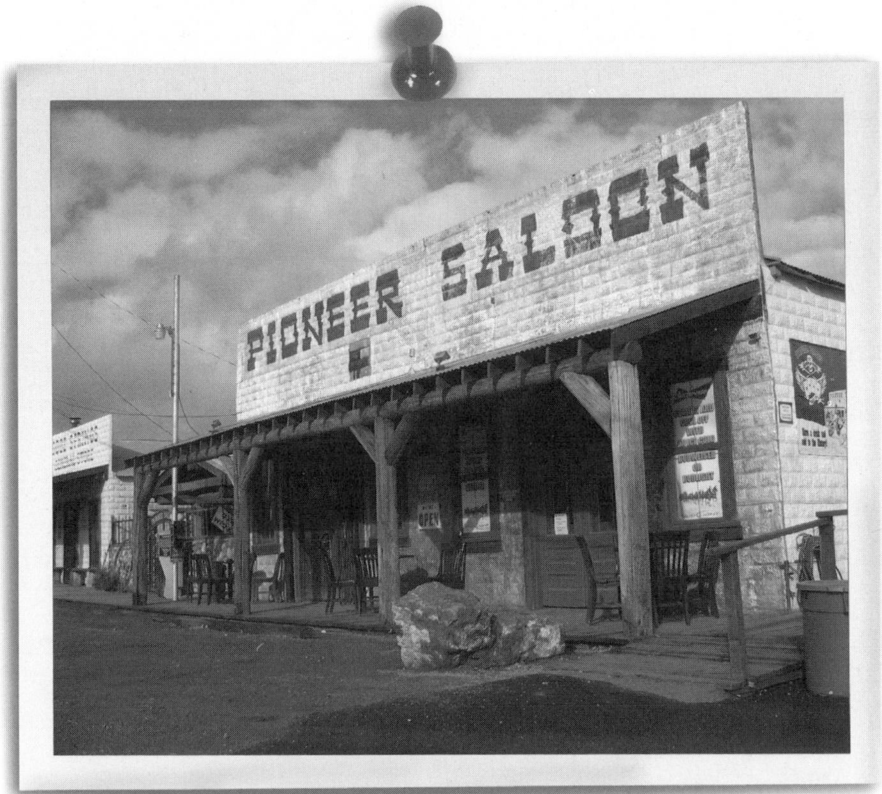

What do Clark Gable and Cheech and Chong have in common? The Pioneer Saloon in Goodsprings.

and foundations of a once-thriving community. But the Pioneer has plenty of life despite its worn appearance, which includes a few bullet holes in the metal walls, a front entrance that was smashed up in 2007 when a driver lost control of his car, and exterior walls that in the early 1980s were painted for a Cheech and Chong comedy (*Things Are Tough All Over*) so that they looked even rustier and shabbier than they normally were.

Inside, the Pioneer boasts a classic cherrywood bar and back-bar, both of which have been there since the place opened. Atop the stove is a melted chunk of aluminum recovered from the site of a tragic airplane crash that claimed the lives of actress Carole Lombard, her mother, and dozens of other passengers in January 1942. Lombard's husband, actor Clark Gable, reportedly sat in the bar for days awaiting word from search crews and then later drowned his sorrow when he learned his wife had died.

Today, Goodsprings, which was a thriving gold-mining town in the early twentieth century, remains an interesting reminder of the region's past. Wandering its dusty, unpaved streets, you can still imagine what southern Nevada was like before theme parks, glitzy hotels, and traffic jams replaced the sand- and sage-covered valleys.

Nevada's Willy Wonka

Henderson

The best part of a visit to the Ethel M Chocolate Factory in Henderson, Nevada, is the end. That's when you're ushered into the lounge and provided with a free sample. Of course, that's not to say the rest of the tour isn't worthwhile. For one thing, it's free. And it's interesting. The story of Ethel M Chocolates began in 1976, when retired seventy-two-year-old candy king Forrest Mars Sr. (creator of M&Ms, Milky Way, Snickers, and other candies) decided to jump back into the confectionery business with a gourmet chocolate label. He specialized in liqueur-filled chocolates, which were originally sold only in Nevada.

Photo courtesy of the Las Vegas News Bureau

The Ethel M Chocolate Factory's garden of succulents.

The company has grown and evolved over the years. Mars died in 1999 at the age of ninety-five, and the company expanded its product line beyond rum- and Kahlúa-filled chocolates to a variety of gourmet treats. In 2005 the company began rebranding its Ethel M retail outlets, which had grown to nineteen in Nevada and Illinois, into Ethel's Chocolate Lounge, an upscale, sit-down dessert cafe that sells chocolate fondue, truffles, tea, chocolates, hot cocoa, and a variety of chocolate-flavored beverages and candies. Plans call for additional lounges to open in other major American cities.

However, the factory, tucked into a suburb of Las Vegas, remains the heart and soul of the company. The Ethel M name lives on in the company's classic collection, including Almond Butter Krisps, Lemon Satin Cremes, Milk Chocolate Raspberry Satin Cremes, and the Ethel M Buttery Pecan Brittle. Visitors to the factory, which is open 8:30 a.m. to 7:00 p.m., can take a self-guided tour that passes by the main candy-making rooms, visible behind glass walls. An overhead video presentation explains that the company uses a special formula to make its gourmet chocolate. According to the tape, Ethel M Chocolates are technically a milk chocolate, although the company incorporates many of the characteristics and flavors associated with dark chocolate. This process results in a richer, more flavorful chocolate. Behind the windows, visitors can see the many machines that mold, shape, fill, and prepare each chocolate. There is something hypnotic about watching hundreds of little, round chocolates marching on a conveyor belt. Naturally, the tour ends inside an Ethel's Chocolate Lounge.

The factory is also home to a giant botanical garden filled with hundreds of species of desert plants, primarily different types of cactus. Spread across two and a half acres, the garden has some 350 different species of cactus, succulents, and desert plants native to the Southwest and various other deserts throughout the world. To someone who's not a cactus expert, this place seems like a prickly Garden of Eden. You can find a wide variety of plants, such as beavertail, purple pancake prickly pears, golden barrels, and saguaros. A series of concrete pathways wind through the Cactus Garden, and interpretive signs describe each plant. Ethel M Chocolates and Cactus Garden is located about 7 miles southeast of the Las Vegas Strip. Drive 5.5 miles east of the Strip on Tropicana Avenue to Mountain Vista. Turn right on Mountain Vista and drive 2 miles to Sunset Way (past the factory). Turn left at the traffic light into Green Valley Business Park, then left again on Cactus Garden Drive.

The Magnet Lady

Henderson

Louise J. Greenfarb of Henderson, Nevada, is a hoarder. Since the 1970s her passion has been refrigerator magnets. At last count, she had acquired more than 35,000 nonduplicated magnets and earned a listing in the *Guinness Book of World Records* for having the world's largest refrigerator magnet collection. For several years, about 7,000 of her magnets were displayed at the Las Vegas Guinness Museum (now closed). Known as "the Magnet Lady" (her license plate is MGNTLDY), she started collecting refrigerator magnets by accident. When her children were young, they would often buy small magnets from vending machines. Worried that they might swallow the little metal and plastic objects, she began putting them on her refrigerator.

"From this time on, it became a growing hobby (or, as my family says, 'obsession') that has never stopped to this day," she noted on her blog. Here husband was in the military, and the family moved all over the world—along the way finding more magnets. In 1989 she and her husband settled in Washington, where friends and others took notice of her collection. She said that stories about her magnet mania began to appear on various TV stations and in newspapers. In the early 1990s she wrote to the *Guinness Book of World Records* to suggest that she might have the world's largest collection of magnets, but she was told that she didn't qualify. Finally, in 1995, Guinness officials reversed themselves and announced that she had made their list of world records. Her collection was mentioned in the next edition of the *Guinness Book of World Records* and profiled in the 1998 version.

Since then, Greenfarb has appeared on national TV shows, including *Maury Povich,* and worked as a consultant for—what else?—a South Korean magnet manufacturer, which wanted her to tell them what type of magnets American consumers might purchase. Her collection includes cartoon figures, sexy magnets, magnetic business cards, ceramic magnets, plastic magnets, sports figure magnets, tourist trap magnets, and many others. She continues to hunt for magnets at garage sales or as free giveaways from merchants. In her home, magnets grace not only the refrigerator but also an assortment of baking sheets, which, it turns out, are perfect magnet holders. In 1997 she told the *Las Vegas Review-Journal* that when she dies, she hopes to be buried in her refrigerator, which would be covered by thousands of her favorite magnets.

Dam Big Place

Hoover Dam

Hoover Dam is just so—*I can't help it*—dam big. In fact, it's difficult to wrap your brain around the—*sorry*—dam thing. It's such a huge chunk of concrete and steel that it boggles the mind to think about

Photo courtesy of the Nevada Commission on Tourism

Contrary to legend, no one is buried in Hoover Dam.

the amount of planning and materials needed to build such a massive structure. The American Society of Civil Engineers once named it one of America's Seven Modern Civil Engineering Wonders. Consider these stats: Built between 1931 and 1934, the dam contains three million cubic yards of concrete, enough to pave a two-lane highway from San Francisco to New York. It rises 726.4 feet high and stretches 1,244 feet across, which makes it larger than the Pyramid of Cheops. Its walls are 660 feet at the thickest part, which is at the bottom (it's shaped like a giant wedge of cheese, with the thickest part down). Each of its 17 generators produces enough power for a city of 65,000 people. Behind the dam is Lake Mead, the largest man-made reservoir in the Western Hemisphere. The lake is 110 miles long, with more than 500 miles of shoreline and a surface area of 274 square miles.

Perhaps the most frequently asked question during dam tours is how many workers were buried inside the dam (*would you call that eternal dam-nation*?). Not a single—*again, sorry*—dam one. The concrete was poured into small wooden-box frames that were only a few feet deep, so anyone falling in would simply have to stand up to avoid being encased in concrete. The tours are worth the effort because they describe the dam's construction and take visitors deep inside to view the massive hydroelectric generators, power transformers, transmission line towers, and other equipment. You also walk 300 feet into a tunnel carved into the canyon wall, through a construction tunnel built in the 1930s, to stand atop a 30-foot-diameter pipe that is filled with water rushing into the generators. There are also some wonderful 1930s design elements, such as terrazzo tile floors that were carefully handcrafted in southwestern Native American designs and sculptor Oskar J. W. Hansen's magnificent Art Deco bronze statues entitled *Winged Figures of the Republic*. In other words, it's a dam fine place to check out.

Nevada's Underwater Ghost Town

Lake Mead

Every couple of decades, a forgotten community seems to rise out of Lake Mead. The town is St. Thomas, a Mormon farming settlement founded in 1865, which was submerged by the waters of Lake Mead after Hoover Dam was built in 1935. However, when the lake level drops, such as during extended drought periods, the ruins of St. Thomas reappear like some modern-day Atlantis.

Mormon farmers established St. Thomas at the confluence of the Muddy and Virgin Rivers in eastern Nevada. Because the Muddy River is fed by artisan springs, it was a reliable water source for growing crops. In the early 1870s the Mormons abandoned St. Thomas as a result of a dispute with the State of Nevada over taxes. The settlers had believed that their community was located in Utah, but an 1870 boundary survey showed it was within Nevada state lines. When Nevada sought two years of back taxes from residents, they returned to Utah. About a decade later, however, the Mormons began to come back to St. Thomas, and soon the town again had several hundred residents.

St. Thomas thrived during the early part of the twentieth century, after the Union Pacific Railroad built a branch through the area and established St. Thomas as a terminus. During World War I St. Thomas became an important shipping point for the local livestock industry as well as for several copper mines in the region. Construction of Hoover Dam, however, brought an end to St. Thomas. The dam's planners decided that the loss of the town was an acceptable trade-off for the project's benefits. Residents (the 1930 census indicated 274 residents) were relocated to the nearby towns of Overton and Logandale. By 1938 the town was underwater.

The walls and foundations of St. Thomas reemerged for the first time in the late 1950s, following a couple of dry years. The lake level rose again, and it wasn't until the late 1990s that St. Thomas reappeared, only to be submerged at the end of the millennium.

Exceptionally dry years in 2002–2007 again dropped the water level, exposing the town once more. Wandering the site during the low-level periods provides glimpses of the old town. In addition to the concrete blocks and foundations, there are skeletal remains of trees. Recent drought years have exposed the ruins for an extended period of time (a fairly packed trail through the muddy flats leads to the town), but the situation can change depending on the season and weather conditions, and Nevada's Mormon Atlantis could easily slip back beneath the murky waters of Lake Mead.

Don Laughlin's Gamble

Laughlin

Minnesotan Don Laughlin arrived in Nevada in the 1950s hoping to make it in the gambling business. For a few years he owned a small club in North Las Vegas. Then, in 1964, he decided to buy a defunct eight-room motel with a diner and bar called Mike's Camp, which sat alongside the Colorado River at the Nevada-Arizona border. The joint had a couple of slot machines, and his idea was to set up a small casino with the slots and a few blackjack table games and intercept some of the highway traffic heading to Las Vegas.

In the early years he and his family lived in part of the motel and rented out four rooms that he had renovated. He named his place Laughlin's Riverside and hit on the idea of offering all-you-can-eat fried-chicken dinners for only 98 cents as a hook for getting people to stop. The little motel-casino with the cheap chicken dinners soon began attracting customers, particularly locals from Bullhead City, Arizona (directly across the river from his place), as well as day gamblers from Needles, California, and Kingman, Arizona. And his place began to grow. By the mid-1980s, Laughlin's success was noticed by other Nevada casino companies, which began building their own places adjacent to his rapidly expanding property. In the late 1960s the U.S. Postal Service agreed to open a post office in the burgeoning community. According to Laughlin, he was asked for a name for

Photo courtesy of the Nevada Commission on Tourism

Laughlin proves that if you build it they will come—and gamble.

the town and suggested "Riverside" or "Casino." The postal official, however, replied that those names were too common and proposed that it be named Laughlin because that was "a good Irish name."

In the town's early days, the shortest way to travel from Bullhead

City to Laughlin was a 15-mile trip over Davis Dam, located north of both communities. In the late 1970s Don Laughlin and other casino owners decided to make it easier for visitors to reach their properties and launched a fleet of free water-taxis to carry passengers from expansive free parking lots on the Arizona side to the casinos on the Nevada side. For a few years the small, covered flat-bottomed motorboats were one of the best free attractions in the state (they still operate, but there is now a fee). In the mid-1980s Laughlin decided that a bridge directly linking the two cities was an even better idea—so he spent $3 million to build one adjacent to his hotel and gave it to the State of Nevada.

The town of Laughlin's rise has been equally remarkable. As recently as 1984, Laughlin counted only ninety-five permanent residents. Today, about 10,000 people live in Laughlin, which is the third-largest gambling destination in the state, outranked only by Las Vegas and Reno. The Laughlin area now includes nine major resort hotels with nearly 11,000 rooms. As for Don Laughlin's Riverside, it has grown to include half a dozen restaurants, a movie theater complex, a bowling alley, a giant RV park, and a car collection that showcases more than seventy rare and historic automobiles (open year-round, with no admission charge).

And even though those cheap all-you-can-eat chicken dinners are a thing of the past, there are a few more guest rooms than there used to be—the place now has 1,404 rooms.

Treasures of the Lost City

Overton

Travelers in southeastern Nevada should try to find the Lost City Museum, a storehouse of history and artifacts related to an ancient and mysterious civilization that disappeared about 1,500 to 2,000 years ago. The museum, located in the tiny enclave of Overton, is housed in a sun-dried, adobe brick building that was erected by the National Park Service in 1935.

Starting in the 1920s, archaeologists have uncovered the ruins of a massive settlement, which they called Pueblo Grande de Nevada, built by the Anasazi people, who lived along the banks of the nearby Virgin and Muddy Rivers. About 800 years ago, the Anasazi abandoned the area for no apparent reason.

The museum was turned over to the State of Nevada in 1953 and has been expanded several times over the years. The last expansion, called the Faye Perkins Wing, was built atop an actual Pueblo foundation that had been excavated in 1935. The site has been reconstructed in such a way as to depict how archaeologists work at a dig site. The Lost City site has provided valuable information about the Anasazi's transition from a nomadic desert tribe, before the time of Christ, to a more sophisticated society that built permanent settle-

You can find the Lost City Museum in Overton.

ments and planted crops. Displays in the museum illustrate the history of the Anasazi.

The museum grounds also house several Pueblo-type structures, made of wattle and daub, which have been reconstructed on original foundations. In addition, there is a replica of a pithouse, which was a covered underground dwelling. Exhibits display hundreds of arrowheads, baskets, *atlatl* (or throwing spears), skins, and pottery. The Lost City Museum (702-397-2193) is located on Route 169 in Overton, about 60 miles northeast of Las Vegas. The museum is open daily from 8:30 a.m. to 4:30 p.m.

Shrine to Desperadoes

Primm

The bullet-riddled 1934 Ford V-8 looks a little out of place inside the modern rotunda that links the Primm Valley Resort to an outlet mall. The Cordoba gray, classic sedan, however, is the Bonnie and Clyde Getaway Car, or Death Car, the vehicle driven by legendary outlaws Bonnie Parker and Clyde Barrow when they were fatally ambushed by law enforcement officials.

The story of Bonnie and Clyde is well documented (including in the award-winning 1967 film *Bonnie and Clyde,* with Warren Beatty and Faye Dunaway). The two met in West Dallas, Texas, early in 1930. Soon, they started a spree of bank robberies, kidnappings, burglaries, and murders throughout the South and Midwest. The FBI and other law enforcement agencies embarked on one of the largest manhunts in U.S. history to capture the couple, who had gained national attention.

Finally, on May 23, 1934, the duo was caught in an ambush on a rural road near Arcadia, Louisiana. Driving a stolen car (the Ford V-8), they stopped to help the father of one of their gang members change a flat tire. Unbeknownst to the outlaws, the man and his flat were a ruse to distract Clyde and force him to drive to the side of the road closest to the awaiting lawmen. As he climbed out of the car, the posse, consisting of six Louisiana and Texas officers, opened fire without warning, instantly killing Clyde. The group continued to fire bullets into the vehicle, in which Bonnie was sitting. It has been estimated that more than two dozen bullets were pumped into each of the bodies, as the officers emptied Browning automatic rifles, shotguns, and pistols during the assault. After Bonnie and Clyde were dead, the lawmen found that the car contained a small arsenal of weapons, including stolen automatic rifles, semiautomatic pistols, handguns, and thousands of rounds of ammunition.

The bullet-pocked Ford, which had been stolen from the Warren family of the nearby Bienville Parish in Louisiana, was eventually returned to its owners, who sold it to a carnival operator. It was shown around the country for several years before being placed on display in a Cincinnati theme park in the 1940s. In 1988 it was sold to Whiskey Pete's Casino, part of the Primm Valley Resort, located on Interstate 15 at the Nevada-California border, about 45 miles west of Las Vegas. The casino's display shows the famous car, as well as historic photos of the Barrow family, the remains of the shirt Clyde was wearing when he died, his handmade mirror, and a belt and necklace he made while in prison.

Desert Sailing

Primm

You're tacking into the wind. The sail billows in the breeze, powering you forward with increasing speed. You are the pilot of this vessel, guiding it across the smooth surface. But it's a smooth surface of sand. And that's what makes landsailing—a sport that might best be described as windsurfing on three wheels—so different from its aquatic counterpart. Landsailing, also known as land yachting, has been around for about half a century, although there are accounts of some cultures in windy, flat desert regions using similar vehicles for regular transportation.

It turns out that Nevada, with its alkali flats and dry lake beds, is prime landsailing territory. These dirt surfers can reach speeds of 60 to 80 miles per hour, depending on conditions. In fact, the world record is 116.7 miles per hour, set on March 20, 1999, on the dry bed of Ivanpah Lake near Primm. The thirty-five-square-mile playa at Ivanpah is a particularly popular landsailing site and host of the annual America's Landsailing Cup Regatta, held each March. The best time of year to hit the Ivanpah flats is between March and October, although most pilots avoid August because it can be dangerously hot.

The typical land yacht has a 12-foot fuselage with a wheel in front and two wheels outrigged in the back. The yachts are generally made of lightweight steel or aluminum tubing and/or fiberglass (with a nylon sail) and accommodate a single rider, although some are two-seaters. Piloting the vehicle is relatively simple: You steer with a foot lever; a main line, controlled with the grip of your hands, controls the sail for adjusting your speed. A typical one-seater costs about $1,800, while the two-seater runs about $2,500. One of the best-known manufacturers is Manta Landsailers of Oakland, California. In the United States, the largest landsailing organization is the North American Land Sailing Association (www.nalsa.org). The sport is also popular in Europe, Australia, and New Zealand.

Naturally, it's the ride that attracts hundreds of enthusiasts. When the wind kicks up and air fills the sail, the vehicle takes off. Soon, the yacht is skimming across the flat desert surface. The yachts are so efficient at using wind power that pilots can go three to four times faster than the wind speed. The optimal wind speed, however, is between 8 and 24 miles per hour. You can buy your own landsailing rig at places like WindPower Sports (www.windpowersports.com) in Las Vegas, or you can take a landsailing excursion. A company called Landsailing Tours (www.golandsailing.com) offers full-day and half-day dirt boat excursions out of Las Vegas and Reno. The cost for a full-day trip, which includes transportation to the sailing site, lunch, beverages, snacks, equipment, and instruction, is $169 per person. A half-day excursion, which doesn't include lunch, is $79 per person.

Photo courtesy of Maria Carr

Ivanpah Dry Lake, near Primm, is one of the world's top landsailing sites.

Handmade by Mother Nature

Red Rock Canyon National Conservation Area

In a place where the great cities of the world have been cloned—Paris, Venice, New York—and anything older than a week has to be considered historic, the coolest thing about the Red Rock Canyon National Conservation Area, located only 12 miles west of downtown Las Vegas, is that it's all natural. What makes the 195,610-acre Red Rock area so spectacular is its geologic formation, which includes large, red sandstone peaks and high, multicolored cliffs. These 3,000-foot-high walls, part of what is known as the Keystone Thrust, are considered unusual because the layers of strata have been turned upside down, meaning the older layers of limestone rock sit atop the younger sandstone rock. This feature is the result of ancient geologic forces—the movement of huge tectonic plates—that about sixty-five million years ago forced the layers of rock to actually flip over, leaving the older stone on top of the younger rock.

In addition to the visually appealing Wilson Cliffs, which are popular with rock climbers, there is Red Rock, which is managed by the federal Bureau of Land Management (BLM). Red Rock has more than a dozen developed hiking and walking trails, a pleasurable 13-mile scenic loop drive, Indian petroglyph sites, the remnants of a sandstone quarry (active about a century ago,) and a BLM visitor center (702-363-1921). The latter, located at the start of the scenic drive, offers detailed maps of the entire area.

Although Red Rock entertains about a million visitors annually, the trails are a good place to avoid the hoi polloi. For instance, one of the easiest walks is the 0.75-mile hike along Lost Creek. The trail begins about 7.5 miles from the visitor center via the scenic drive. After parking in a marked area, you can begin walking beside Lost Creek, a trickling permanent stream. The trail passes beautiful sandstone cliffs before ending in a box canyon with no outlet. During the spring the canyon contains a pleasant waterfall.

Photo courtesy of the Nevada Commission on Tourism

Red Rock Canyon National Conservation Area offers, well, lots of red rocks (and other colors).

An equally scenic hike is the 3-mile (round-trip) walk along Pine Creek Trail, which is accessed from the Pine Creek Canyon Overlook, located about 10.5 miles from the visitor center. From the trailhead, the route slants downward to join a closed dirt road that leads to the ruins of the Horace Wilson homestead (a pioneer family in the area). Above the abandoned ranch site, where only foundations remain, the road splits, and you should go left. Soon the trail enters a small stand of large ponderosa pine trees, which give the trail its name. Ponderosa pines rarely grow at this elevation in the desert—they are normally found in much higher and moister climates. You also pass spiky agave plants, juniper, and the ubiquitous sagebrush. The trail winds through sandstone walls that are streaked with black desert varnish before it ends in the rocks near a streambed (it has water most of the year). You can continue hiking for another mile by following the stream's path deeper into the canyon.

For a different perspective, the 3-mile (round-trip) Keystone Thrust Trail offers an opportunity to study the unique geologic events that helped create Red Rock Canyon. The trailhead is located at the lower White Rock Spring parking area. From the parking lot, follow a dirt road for nearly half a mile. Turn right (east) on another dirt road and continue for 0.75 mile to a fork. Follow the right branch into a small canyon that leads to the Keystone Thrust Fault. At the fault you can clearly see the fracturing and upthrusting that make Red Rock Canyon so geologically fascinating. The trail offers spectacular views of the surrounding area, but the lack of trees means there is no shade. The presence of seasonal water and vegetation in Red Rock supports a rich variety of animal species. Sometimes, with binoculars and a bit of luck, you can spot bighorn sheep, bobcats, gray foxes, and even wild burros at the higher elevations.

What's in a Name?

Searchlight

Depending on what version of the story you hear, the old mining town of Searchlight, located 55 miles south of Las Vegas on U.S. Highway 95, was named after a popular brand of wooden matches, in honor of a miner named Lloyd Searchlight, or by one of the town's earliest prospectors, who allegedly quipped that it would take a searchlight to find any gold in the region. All three stories have appeared in various history books over the years. However, one of the town's native sons, U.S. senator Harry Reid, who was born in Searchlight in 1939, has written a history of his hometown and concluded that the latter tale is most likely the truth.

Searchlight may or may not have been named after a box of matches.

In his book *Searchlight: The Camp That Didn't Fail,* Reid reveals that he could find no evidence of any miner named Lloyd Searchlight. It also appears that the tale of the town's being named after the Searchlight brand of wooden matches was most likely the fanciful concoction of a descendant of one of the town's founders. Reid's research, however, did show that Searchlight most probably got its name when one of the town's first residents, prospector George Colton, remarked that there was gold in the area but it would take a searchlight to find it.

Searchlight traces its beginnings to about May 1897, with the discovery of gold in the area. By July 1898 the Searchlight mining district had been formed, and a small tent camp was cropping up in the desert. By 1902 Searchlight had a post office, a 15-mile-long narrow-gauge railroad linking the mines to a mill on the Colorado River, a newspaper, stores, and saloons. In 1907 the population reached its peak at several thousand people, although exact numbers are difficult to determine because of the transient nature of mining towns. A year later, ambitious town boosters took a stab at being named the seat of the newly formed Clark County but lost out to Las Vegas, which at the time was actually smaller than Searchlight.

Searchlight's fortunes, however, were intertwined with the state of its mining industry, and when the ore began to fade after 1916, the town, too, started to decline. By the 1930 census, only 137 people still lived in Searchlight. Today, the community has nearly 1,000 residents, many of them retirees escaping the hustle and bustle of bigger cities. The main reminders of the town's mining past are a few worn wooden mining headframes still standing on the hills surrounding the town, as well as the Searchlight Historic Museum, which is easy to spot because it has a large wooden headframe in front. Built in 1904, the derricklike structure was used at Searchlight's Ruth Elder mine.

Searchlight's other main attraction is the Searchlight Nugget, a small neighborhood-style casino with a restaurant that offers something not found in too many places these days—a 10-cent cup of coffee. Amazingly, the Nugget also offers free refills on that cheap cup of joe.

Now that's something that would take a searchlight to find anywhere else.

From Outlaws to Eccentrics

Spring Mountain Ranch State Park

Spring Mountain Ranch State Park (702-875-4141) has seen it all. Located 15 miles west of Las Vegas, the park is nestled at the base of the colorfully banded Wilson Cliffs, part of the Red Rock Canyon area. In addition to being one of the most scenic places in southern Nevada, the site was originally a hideout for robbers, who preyed on pack trains traveling on the Old Spanish Trail, which passed nearby. In 1864 an outlaw named Bill Williams claimed the area and maintained horses at the site, which had plentiful water and grass. In the mid-1870s James Wilson and his partner, George Anderson, filed for legal ownership of the site, which they named Sand Stone Ranch. Anderson departed in the early 1880s, and Wilson assumed control of the property and also adopted and raised Anderson's two sons. The two, Jim Wilson Jr. and Tweed, inherited the ranch after their stepfather died in 1906.

The two operated the spread for many years before selling it in 1929 to Willard George, a family friend, who allowed them to live on the ranch until they died. They are buried, with their adopted father, in a small cemetery on the ranch. George began to develop the ranch, adding a chinchilla farm (he was a Hollywood furrier by trade) as well as cattle. In 1944 George leased the ranch to actor Chester Lauck ("Lum" from the *Lum and Abner* radio show), the first of the ranch's celebrity owners. Lauck purchased the property in 1948 and constructed an impressive New England–style cut sandstone and redwood ranch house. Lauck used the ranch, called the Bar Nothing Ranch, as a vacation retreat and summer camp for boys, while raising cattle on the land.

Beautiful Spring Mountain Ranch State Park offers a bucolic setting beyond the neon lights of Las Vegas.

In 1955 Lauck sold the ranch estate to Vera Krupp, wife of the German munitions manufacturer Alfried Krupp. Mrs. Krupp added a swimming pool and expanded the house and the cattle operations. Making the ranch her principal residence, she renamed it Spring Mountain Ranch. With its beautifully manicured meadows and cool shade from the southern Nevada heat, the ranch was a popular retreat for Mrs. Krupp's celebrity friends. The property was sold in 1967 to the Hughes Tool Company, which was part of the Howard Hughes empire. Although Hughes never lived at the ranch, executives of his Summa Corporation were allowed to stay there. In 1972 two southern Nevada businessmen, Fletcher Jones and William Murphy, bought the ranch and announced plans to construct a large housing development. Public outcry resulted in the estate's being sold in 1974 to the Nevada Division of State Parks.

Today, the ranch continues to be used as a working cattle ranch. It's not uncommon to see several dozen cows grazing on the pastures surrounding the sprawling ranch-style main house, which is open for tours. In addition, guided tours of the park's 520 acres are offered on weekends. This tour includes a visit to the Old Reservoir, the Wilson family cemetery, an 1880s board and batten cabin, an 1864 stone cabin and blacksmith shop, and other ranch buildings. The park's expansive picnic grounds are open daily. The park, open daily from 8:00 a.m. until dusk, is also a popular location for outdoor concerts in the spring and summer months.

The Land of Mutant Rocks

Valley of Fire State Park

There are some strange stones at Valley of Fire State Park. One, called Elephant Rock, resembles a pachyderm with thick legs and a long trunk. In another part of the park are the Beehives, several large, round sandstone formations scored with concentric cracks and lines that make them resemble stone hives. And then there are the Seven Sisters, a row of massive red sandstone pillars; Piano Rock, which looks like an upright piano; Poodle Rock, which bears a strong resemblance to that canine's distinctive head; and Duck Rock, which, of course, takes after a duck. The park is also home to a significant collection of prehistoric petroglyphs.

Geologists say that erosion created this sandstone sculpture garden. The sandstone traces its origins to about 150 million years ago, when the area was largely shifting sand dunes. The sand eventually turned into stone, which over the centuries has been carved by the wind and rain into such a wide variety of evocative shapes. The distinctive red-colored sandstone is the result of oxidized iron that permeated the rock. Archaeological evidence indicates that the valley has long fascinated people. Among the earliest inhabitants were

Photo courtesy of the Nevada Commission on Tourism

Weird formations can be found at Valley of Fire State Park.

the Basketmaker people and the Anasazi Pueblo farmers from the nearby Moapa Valley. Proof of their presence in the valley can be found among the many petroglyphs (prehistoric Indian rock writings) on the valley walls. For example, in Petroglyph Canyon, north of the visitor center, the walls are lined with glyphs such as kachina figures (considered a rare image), drawings of dancers holding hands, footprints, and curved lines. The canyon trail leads to another landmark, Mouse's Tank, a large rock catch basin called a *tinaja*. This particular stone bowl provided a regular source of water for birds, animals, and, in the 1890s, an outlaw Indian (named Mouse) who hid in the area. At Atlatl Rock visitors will find a large collection of petroglyphs carved high on the side of a massive rock mound. Metal walkways lead to the carvings, which include an atlatl (an ancient spear-throwing stick), bighorn sheep, and a variety of other symbols.

The park visitor center (702-397-2088), which is open daily from 8:30 a.m. to 4:30 p.m., is a good place to begin a visit. In addition to being the only place within miles to find a water fountain, the center offers exhibits about the geology and animal life of the region, including the rare and protected desert tortoise. The center also has good information about desert flora and fauna. Because of its location, the Valley of Fire is one of the best places in the state to watch wildflowers bloom. In late March and early April, depending on rainfall, the park roads offer good places to spot the springtime blooms of desert marigold, indigobush, and desert mallow.

The Valley of Fire has two campgrounds (both just off the main road, west of the visitor center) with fifty campsites. The sites are equipped with shaded tables, barbecue grills, water, and restrooms. There is also a recreational vehicle dump station near the campgrounds. Valley of Fire State Park is located about 50 miles northeast of Las Vegas. From Las Vegas travel east on Interstate 15 to Route 169. Head south on 169 for 24 miles to the park.

Then, just look for the elephant, the piano, the poodle, or the duck.

CHAPTER

3

East

The Forgotten Nevada

"Some people are malicious enough to think that if the devil were set at liberty and told to confine himself to Nevada Territory, that he would come here and loaf sadly around, awhile, and then get homesick and go back to hell again."

—Mark Twain, in a letter (1862)

In the eastern *part of Nevada, much of the landscape is vast and seemingly vacant, and the communities are spaced far apart. All that emptiness affects people in different ways. Some find it unsettling and disturbing, and they can't wait to drive through it as quickly as possible. Others see beauty in the desert and its subtle colors and tones. At least a few are attracted to the wide-open environment and crave the elbow room, the solitude, and the freedom. An artist might look at the land as a canvas to be worked, a tabula rasa—a blank slate—just waiting to be shaped into something else. A miner, on the other hand, sees potential under the ground and tries to rearrange the land so that it will relinquish its wealth. In the end, it all depends on what you're looking for.*

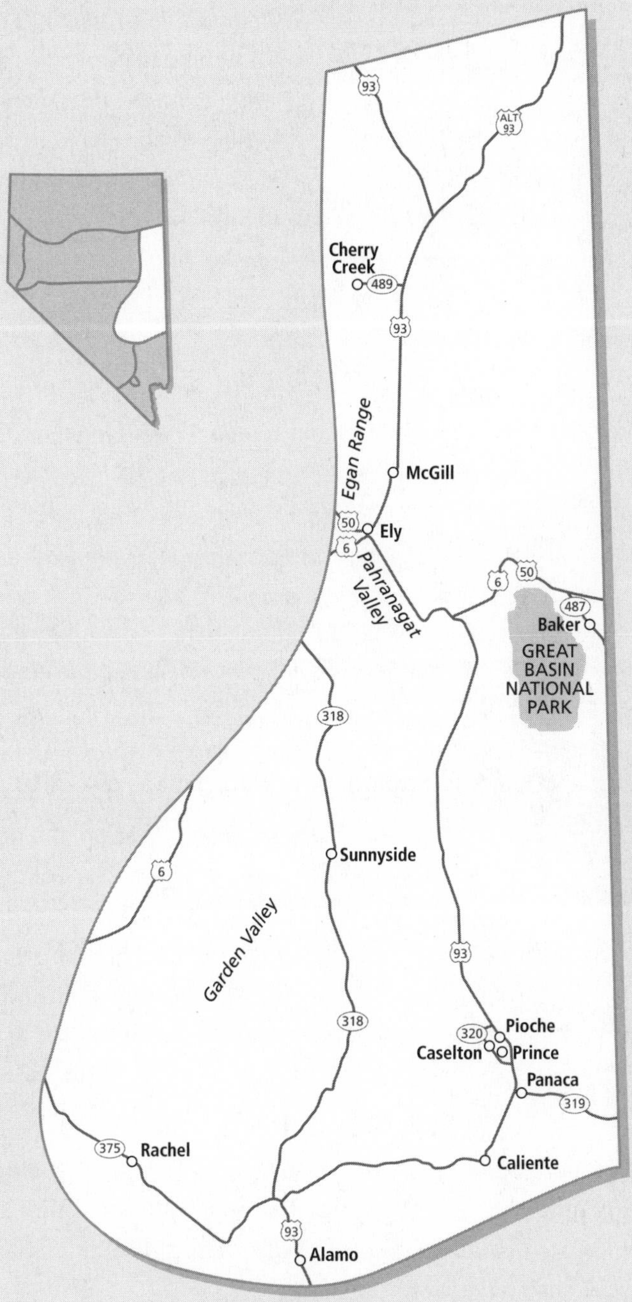
93
ALT 93
Cherry Creek
489
93
Egan Range
McGill
50
Ely
6
Pahranagat Valley
6
50
487
Baker
GREAT BASIN NATIONAL PARK
318
Sunnyside
6
Garden Valley
93
318
Pioche
320
Caselton
Prince
Panaca
319
375
Rachel
Caliente
93
Alamo

East

The Permanent Wave Society

Nevadans can be an artistic lot. When the muse hits, they're capable of turning nearly anything into a thing of beauty (keeping in mind that beauty is, of course, quite subjective). That explains such things as the unusual displays of public art found along Route 488, the road leading from the tiny settlement of Baker to the entrance to Great Basin National Park. There, seemingly spontaneous outbursts of artistic expression can be found along the posts lining the route. In fact, locals like to joke that the fence art is "post-impressionist."

Apparently, the impetus for this creativity was the late "Doc" Sherman, a Baker resident and artist, who, in a bit of whimsy in the mid-1990s, attached rubber gloves filled with cement to the top of a fence post. He named his waving handiwork *The Permanent Wave,* which gave birth to the Permanent Wave Society, a sort of loose-knit coalition of friends and neighbors who have added additional pieces of artwork to the fence. Over the years several dozen art objects have been placed on or near the fence. Many, like the rusting hulk of an old automobile driven by the skeleton of a horse, known as *Horse with No Name,* are definitely eye-catching. Others rely on visual humor or puns, such as the head of an alien space creature holding a ski; a large rubber dinosaur wearing a bib and holding a fork; and a wooden face with CDs for its eyes, nose, and mouth and an eye patch, which is titled *CD Character*.

Post-impressionist art by Baker's Permanent Wave Society: wave as you go by.

"Doc" Sherman, who began creating his work as therapy after being partially paralyzed by a stroke, passed away in 2004, but other local artists have tried to keep the spirit of the society alive by freshening up his work and adding new ones.

All Aboard

Caliente

The most noticeable thing about the town of Caliente is the size of its train depot. The two-story, mission-style structure, built in 1923, overpowers the rest of the community. Adjacent to the town's 2-block-long commercial district, the depot building illustrates the high hopes that the Union Pacific Railroad had for the community. Named for natural hot springs in the area, Caliente (Spanish for "hot") was originally part of a large ranch established in the early 1860s. In 1901 the Union Pacific Railroad established the town as a

Caliente's Depot has always been larger than life.

railroad division point and erected an engine house and other facilities. About this time, the railroad built a row of neat, nearly identical houses beside the tracks for its workers; eighteen of the quaint cottages remain standing.

In 1923 the railroad constructed the depot, which included a train station, telegraph office, restaurant, and hotel. Regular train service to Caliente ceased in the 1980s. More recently, the depot has been restored and used for city offices, the town library, an art gallery, and a community center. Other reminders of the town's railroad roots include several historic buildings in the commercial row district, such as the former Train Service Store, also dating to the 1920s, and the Cornelius/Scott Hotel, a three-story stucco building erected in 1928 for overnight passengers. Reportedly, one of its guests was President Herbert Hoover, who apparently slept or dined in nearly as many places in eastern Nevada (if you believe all the claims made by various hotels) as George Washington is said to have done in the colonial states.

The "Not Open" Cafe

Caselton

The legacy of Gue Gim "Missy" Wah's homemade Chinese-American dishes has survived long after she died more than two decades ago. Indeed, it's a matter of pride among longtime Nevadans to be able to claim that they had enjoyed one of her legendary meals. Wah was born in Lin Lun Li, China, in 1900. Her father, Ng Louie Der, immigrated to San Francisco in 1870 or 1880, where he established a successful business in that city's Chinatown. He had left a wife behind but was able to travel between the United States and China to visit her; as a result she bore him five children, including Gue Gim.

In 1912 Gue Gim moved to San Francisco to live with her father. As was custom at the time, her family had her marry Tom Fook Wah, a man who was twenty-nine years her senior. Wah brought her to the remote mining camp of Prince, Nevada, near Caselton, where he ran a boardinghouse and restaurant. In 1933 Tom Wah became seriously ill with cancer and died. Gue Gim took over the boardinghouse and restaurant, which gained a loyal following, including—surprise!—former president Herbert Hoover, who had mining interests in the region.

After World War II most of the mines in the Prince-Caselton area closed, and the settlement became a virtual ghost town—except for Gue Gim's restaurant. During the next several decades, her reputation as an outstanding cook spread throughout southern Nevada. Because help was difficult to find, Gue Gim did all the cooking herself, using seasonings and herbs from her own garden, and required advance reservations before she would even begin to prepare a meal. Her quirky "Not Open" cafe, as it was called in a 1980 issue of *Nevada Magazine,* became known as one of the state's most exclusive eateries. Later that year, she was honored as the grand marshal of the annual Nevada Day Parade in Carson City, and one Reno columnist wrote she was "a little bit of a woman with a great big heart, a heap of courage and a fascinating background."

At the age of eighty-five, she finally decided to hang up her skillet for good. She died in her home in the ghost town of Prince on June 15, 1988, and was buried in nearby Pioche.

Jailhouse Blues

Cherry Creek

Somebody in the old mining town of Cherry Creek had a macabre sense of humor. On a hill south of the near-ghost town are the local cemeteries. Segregated by religious and ethnic identity, each contains dozens of worn wooden markers and elegant marble tombstones and monuments. Adjacent to these fields of everlasting dreams is a decrepit, single-story log cabin building. On a small sign affixed to the building, above the front door, is the word JAIL. The

Photo courtesy of the Nevada Commission on Tourism

These days, Cherry Creek boasts more ghosts than people.

unlikely coincidence of having a jail so close to the cemeteries is certainly enough to make one think twice about a life of crime.

The best place to learn Cherry Creek's story is the former Cherry Creek Schoolhouse, now a small local museum. Open during the summer and by appointment, the museum has an assortment of antiques, old bicycles, mining tools, and furniture collected from the area. The town, located about 50 miles north of Ely, has a rich history that began with the discovery of gold and silver in about 1872. Within a short time, more than 1,000 miners and others had flocked to the new, hot mining camp of the moment. For the next several decades, the mines of Cherry Creek (named for chokecherry bushes in the area) experienced the usual cyclical booms and busts of a mining town.

By the mid-twentieth century, however, Cherry Creek had settled into a state of quiet inactivity. Visitors will find a handful of buildings scattered around the town site, including a large red freight barn and the Cherry Creek Barrel Saloon (open in the summer), a saloon with considerable rustic charm. Adjacent to the red barn are the impressive remains of several stone buildings, reminders of a rather substantial business district once located there.

Stone Hives and a Yurt

Egan Range

Out on the edge of the Egan Range, about 12 miles south of Ely, are half a dozen 30-foot-high rock domes that are 27 feet around at the base. Although they might appear to have been made by giant bees, they're actually stone charcoal ovens erected in 1876. Known as the Ward Charcoal Ovens, they converted wood into hotter-burning charcoal, which was used to heat local mining smelters. Each of the rock kilns was layered with about thirty-five cords of wood, usually piñon pine and juniper, which were partially burned to produce the charcoal. The wood was trimmed into 6-foot lengths and stacked vertically inside the dome, with access through the floor opening. Additional wood was loaded into the oven from an upper opening. The wood was ignited, and metal doors were sealed shut at the openings. Small vents at the base of the ovens were opened and closed to control the heat and the amount of air. According to accounts, it took nine to eleven days to slow-burn the wood into charcoal. At the end, water was poured through the chimney to extinguish the smoldering wood, which was then loaded into sacks.

The ovens were constructed because valuable gold and silver ore had been discovered in the foothills of Ward Mountain in 1872. Within three years Ward had become one of the largest communities in eastern Nevada, with a population of more than 1,000. But three years later, the mines had begun to shut down, and the population quickly dropped. For the next few decades, mining efforts continued

Photo courtesy of the Nevada Commission on Tourism

The Ward Charcoal Ovens are a hot historical attraction.

sporadically, but by the early twentieth century Ward was a ghost town. The mighty ovens, built a couple of miles from the town site, were abandoned within a few years of being built.

During the next century the big cone-shaped structures aged fairly gracefully. At times they were put to use to stable horses and converted into emergency lodging for wandering sheepherders and cowboys. According to one local legend, the interior of one was painted white, and a bed was hauled inside so that it could serve as a honeymoon suite for a gambler and his fiancée. However, the couple apparently quarreled and called off the wedding—probably because she didn't want to spend the most important night of her life in a drafty old charcoal oven.

In the mid-twentieth century, the ovens were acquired by the Nevada Division of State Parks, which added picnic tables and a handful of undeveloped campsites. The site is open daily throughout the year from sunrise to sunset. The division also developed a series of hiking trails into the surrounding Egan Range, which includes Ward Mountain. More recently, park staff erected the state's only yurt hut a few miles from the ovens. The round, fabric tent with a wood-lattice frame and plywood floor—the traditional dwelling of nomadic people who live on the cold, barren steppes of Central Asia—is available for overnight camping. To make a reservation contact the park at wardcharcoalovens@sbcglobal.net.

Make Tracks to This Old Train

Ely

There's something to be said for never tossing anything out. For example, the Nevada Northern Railway in Ely is considered one of the most intact and well-preserved short-line railroads in the country because over the years its owners held on to practically every scrap of paper and piece of equipment.

Nearly everything appears much as it did during the Nevada Northern's heyday. Wandering through the Nevada Northern Railway is like being in a time warp. From the oak rolltop desks to the dirt-floor blacksmith shop, the place is pretty much the way it was during the eighty years that the Nevada Northern was operating. There's a sense that the railroad is still operating—that everyone just went home for the weekend and is coming back on Monday. The desks, the filing cabinets, and even the black ceramic telephones in the depot building are original—they were installed when the railroad was built in 1906. The railroad never replaced or removed anything.

The guided tour usually begins with a walk through the two-story East Ely Depot building, the centerpiece of the museum. Inside, visitors will find elegant antique wood-and-brass ticket windows, benches, and light fixtures. At the Transportation Building several Nevada Northern

Get railroaded in Ely with Nevada Northern Railway's Engine Number 40. (Photo courtesy of Nevada Commission on Tourism)

locomotives are on display, such as a rare 1907 steam-powered rotary snowplow; a massive steam-powered crane, also built in 1907; and the handsome steam ten-wheel Baldwin locomotive, Number 40—called the "Ghost Train of Old Ely"—which was built in 1910 and rebuilt several years ago. Other buildings house many of the fifty or so pieces of rolling stock owned by the museum, including early-twentieth-century ore cars, flatcars, cabooses, and a 1917 coach car that was converted into a rolling bunkhouse for mine workers.

The railroad was established by the Nevada Consolidated Copper Company (which later became part of the Kennecott Copper Company) to transport ore from the copper mines in Copper Flat, west of Ely, to a large smelter in McGill, 9 miles northeast of Ely. After the ore was processed, the copper was carried by the railroad to the Southern Pacific Railroad line at Cobre, located 130 miles north of Ely. The railroad operated until 1983, when the copper mines were shut down.

After the train line ceased operating, the mining company donated all the rolling stock, buildings, tracks, equipment, and land to the city of Ely. The railroad's depot and several buildings were turned over to the Nevada State Museum to manage, and a nonprofit foundation was created to operate the train as a tourist railroad. These days, thousands of rail fans travel to Ely annually to ride on the vintage train and explore the restored depot, maintenance buildings, and other structures. Train rides are offered in the summer months and on selected weekends. For more information, call (775) 289-2085 or visit www.nevadanorthernrailway.net. A unique opportunity offered by the railroad is to actually rent the train. For a fee, you can play engineer by learning how to pilot the train around the yard or on one of the excursion routes.

Choo. Choo.

Painting the Town Red (and Other Colors)

Ely

Murals on buildings aren't anything especially new, but the town of Ely has taken wall-size paintings to a new level. In the last couple of years, more than twenty building walls in the former copper-mining center have been transformed from blank brick or concrete surfaces to works of art. Ely's mural project began in 1999, when local businessman Norm Goeringer hired Nevada cowboy artist Larry Bute to paint a giant mural titled *Cattle Drive*. The mural depicts the local Nevada Northern Railway locomotive and a cattle drive on the side of Goeringer's building located on the corner of Aultman and Fourth

Streets. Other local businesses took note, and several commissioned Bute to paint western murals on their buildings. Eventually, a non-profit group called the Ely Renaissance Society formed and began raising money to transform empty walls into huge murals.

Supporters of the mural project point to the town of Chemainus, British Columbia, as inspiration. There, more than thirty murals have been painted on local buildings and have helped revitalize a decaying lumber town. Similarly, Ely has experienced considerable economic turmoil as its once-thriving copper-mining industry faded in the 1980s. The murals have become a way to help Ely attract attention and, it hopes, tourists. In 2004 Ely's murals helped the town host the Global Mural Conference, which brought about a hundred mural artists and community arts and culture experts to town for several days of meetings and workshops.

Photo courtesy of the Nevada Commission on Tourism

What do you call a colorful painting on the wall of an old building? Art, of course.

Wandering the streets of Ely, visitors can easily spot the town's signature murals. Most have western themes that reflect historical events or scenes representative of the area's past as a ranching and mining center. Bute has painted several of the murals, but other artists have also contributed, including Wei Luan, Paul Ygartua, Don and Jared Gray, and Colin Williams, as well as Ely artists Chris Kreider and Don Cates. A walking tour of the murals is like leafing through a photo album of the community's roots.

The first mural commissioned by the Ely Renaissance Society, dedicated in 2000, is a patriotic scene showing an early-twentieth-century Fourth of July celebration. Titled *4th of July Celebration,* the mural can be found on a building at 2000 Aultman Street. At 201 High Street, Bute painted a re-creation of an old-time blacksmith shop called, naturally, *The Blacksmith Shop*. The mural faces the spot where there once was a blacksmith shop. Ygartua's mural *United by Our Children,* located on a building at the corner of Aultman and Great Basin Boulevard, shows local children representing the various ethnic groups that have settled in the Ely area over the years. *Liberty Pit,* on the corner of Aultman and Fourth Streets, is a historic interpretation of the Liberty Pit copper mine. The workers in this mural painted by Wei Luan represent various ethnic groups that came to Ely to work in the mines.

Art That Makes a Really Big Statement

Garden Valley

Artist Michael Heizer doesn't talk about his work (in the past thirty years, he's agreed to only two interviews with the *New York Times*). However, his magnum opus, which he's been working on since 1971, speaks volumes. Called *City,* the project is earthen art of unprecedented size—it covers a space about 1.25 miles long and more than 0.25 mile wide—and is one of the largest sculptures ever made. Heizer is an environmental artist who specializes in creating works in the natural world. With *City,* he is using concrete, rock, and massive mounds of dirt to craft a work designed to rival the Native American mounds of the Midwest or the ancient cities of Central and South America.

In 1999 Heizer told *New York Times* writer Michael Kimmelman that he came up with the idea for *City* in 1970, after he had spent time in the Yucatán studying Chichen Itza. He had already established himself at the forefront of the art movement that became known as Land Art, Earth Art, or Environmental Art. In 1969 he had completed *Double Negative,* a 1,500-foot-long, 50-foot-deep, 30-foot-wide slice gouged out of a mesa near Overton, Nevada.

With *City,* Heizer envisioned a series of "complexes," with each containing mounds and structures spread over hundreds of acres and some reaching 80 feet high. After scouting around, he selected the remote Garden Valley in eastern Nevada—about two hours from the nearest paved road—because he could afford the amount of land there he needed to create his masterpiece. A fan Web site devoted to Heizer's work (http://doublenegative.tarasen.net/city.html) quotes the artist as saying, "As long as you're going to make a sculpture, why not make one that competes with a 747, or the Empire State Building, the Golden Gate Bridge." Working mostly by himself, Heizer completed *Complex 1* in the late 1970s. He began work on the next two complexes but found it slow going because of limited financial resources. In the late 1990s two private art foundations agreed to fund completion of *City*. Since then, the Dia Art Foundation has funneled millions of dollars in grants to the project, which, according to some reports, may finally be completed by 2010.

In the meantime, few have ever actually seen *City*. Heizer does not allow visitors—he says he'll have them arrested or shot—citing safety and liability issues as well as a desire to have the public view it only when it is completed. As Heizer told Kimmelman in 1999, "All these rubberneckers show up as if it's entertainment. People fly over the place. This is private property. People presume that I want them to see it. That is a rash presumption. . . . The work isn't cohesive yet. When I finish Phase 5, O.K."

Heizer's project gained unwanted attention in 2004 when the Department of Energy announced plans to construct a railroad to transport nuclear waste from Caliente to the Yucca Mountain Nuclear Waste Repository. According to the American Association of Museum Directors, which joined Heizer to oppose building the railroad, the proposed rail line would "permanently destroy a visitor's experience of Heizer's isolated sculpture by causing irrevocable harm to the Valley's undisturbed emptiness and the silence of its delicate desert environment."

The Great, Great Basin National Park

Great Basin National Park

Encompassing 13,063-foot Wheeler Peak, groves of ancient bristlecone pine trees, a desert glacier, a massive limestone arch, and more than half a mile of limestone caves filled with fascinating formations, Great Basin National Park manages to fit quite a lot into its 77,000 acres. Created to celebrate the Great Basin, a vast area of wide, long valleys separated by dozens of mountain ranges, the park is five miles west of Baker and includes portions of Utah, Oregon, Idaho, and Nevada. Explorer John C. Frémont named the region after noticing that its rivers do not flow to the ocean but rather drain inland into lakes and sinks (dry lake beds), like a giant basin.

Great Basin National Park, ironically, doesn't include much basin and is mostly range. The park takes in a chunk of the Snake Range, including a handful of peaks that rise more than 10,000 feet, including Wheeler Peak (at 13,063 feet, the largest peak entirely located in Nevada), Baker Peak (12,298 feet), Mount Washington (11,676 feet), Lincoln Peak (11,597 feet), and Pyramid Peak (11,921 feet). Because of the wide range in elevations found in the park, it contains seven of the eight ecosystems of the Great Basin. Plant and animal life zones extend upward from sagebrush desert, characterized by jackrabbits, sagebrush, and cacti, to treeless alpine, home to golden eagles, ravens, holmgren buckwheat, and the endangered Nevada primrose.

Trivia

Death of the World's Oldest Thing

In 1964 Donald R. Currey, a geology doctoral student at the University of North Carolina, was given permission by the U.S. Forest Service to study the bristlecone pines growing in a grove at the base of Wheeler Peak in eastern Nevada. Currey was particularly interested in studying the rings inside these ancient trees, which had been discovered only a few years earlier. Researchers had identified bristlecones in the White Mountains of California as being as ancient as 4,000 years old. Currey's research specialty was Ice Age glaciers, and he hoped that bristlecone tree rings might provide some insights about the conditions in prehistoric times. One of the trees in the Wheeler Peak grove appeared to be extremely old, and it was Currey's desire to extract tree rings that could help him with his research. Most trees, including bristlecone pines, add a ring for each year they grow. Scientists study variations in the width of the rings to determine patterns of good and bad growing seasons during past years. The rings literally serve as a record of the lifetime of the tree and are useful in the study of climate changes.

The Forest Service permitted Currey not only to take core samples from several of the oldest-looking bristlecone trees but also to cut down one of his choosing to examine its growth rings. Bristlecone trees grow in a kind of twisted way, which sometimes makes it difficult to locate the oldest part of the tree in a core sample. The living tree that Currey chose to remove, which later became known as "Prometheus," appeared to be a good candidate. It

Photo courtesy of the Nevada Commission on Tourism

Bristlecone pines are older than most Las Vegas lounge acts.

was one of the largest and oldest-looking trees in the grove and seemed as though it would contain a large number of growth rings.

Although some of the Forest Service staff expressed reservations about cutting such an old tree, Currey was given the go-ahead, and the tree was chopped down using a chain saw. Currey began counting the growth rings, which numbered about 4,900. Because every ring represents a year, it meant that the tree was nearly 5,000 years old. Later, it was determined that Prometheus had been the oldest known living tree in the world.

Or at least it was until it was cut down.

Great Basin National Park boasts a glacier in the desert.

What makes the park special is such features as Lehman Caves, a series of underground passages filled with limestone formations, the giant stone Lexington Arch, and groves of bristlecone pine trees, which are among the world's oldest living things. Lehman Caves, which are open for guided tours, are a labyrinth of subterranean chambers lined with stalactites and stalagmites that extend for about 0.6 mile. A Mormon farmer, Absalom Lehman, discovered the caves in 1885 and soon began offering tours. In 1922 they were declared a national monument.

The park includes several campgrounds, miles of hiking trails, and a 12-mile scenic drive from the visitor center to a trailhead at the base of Wheeler Peak. The Bristlecone Trail, which begins there, is a 3-mile round-trip journey from the Wheeler Peak Campground to one of the park's largest groves of bristlecone pine trees. Bristlecone pines can live for thousands of years because of the properties of their concentrated tree resin. The wood of the bristlecone is also extremely dense and hard, making it very resistant to insects, the elements, and old age. The oldest bristlecone discovered in Nevada was more than 4,900 years old. Rangers believe that several bristlecones at Great Basin Park are more than 4,000 years old. From the end of the Bristlecone Trail, you can also continue on the Glacier Trail, a 2-mile climb to a glacier that is tucked into a scenic cirque at the base of Wheeler Peak. This field of ice, which stays frozen throughout the year, is the only glacial remnant in the state.

Another of the park's major features is Lexington Arch, a natural limestone bridge that is more than six stories high. Located near the park's southeastern boundary, Lexington Arch is believed to have once been part of a limestone cave. Over the centuries, the cave's rock walls eroded away, leaving only the arch, which is thought to have been the cave's entrance.

For more information about Great Basin National Park, call the park's information line at (775) 234-7331 or go to the park's Web site at www.nps.gov/grba.

A Place Where Everybody Knows Your Name

McGill

The McGill Club is a funky, smoky, old-time watering hole that boasts a massive wooden back-bar that is a century old—and dust that seems at least as old. But nobody goes to the McGill Club to admire its housekeeping. Folks stop in because the saloon has character and history, and because there aren't too many places like it in this world of cookie-cutter lounges and sports bars. For example, one of the highlights of a visit to the joint is viewing the patriotic display of

Dorian Gray Shops Here

Imagine a drugstore in a remote rural town, where the longtime owner dies and his widow tries to keep it open for a while and then decides to lock up the shop. For years it sits there, fully stocked and ready for business—but not open. Tubes of Ipana toothpaste, jars of Dippity-Do hair gel, and other nearly forgotten brand names fill the shelves. That's essentially what happened to the McGill Drug Store in the old mining town of McGill. The apothecary store opened in 1915 and operated continuously for the next sixty-four years. From 1950 to 1979, the owners were Gerald and Elsa Culbert, who filled prescriptions, maintained a soda fountain in the back, and sold a wide variety of sundries and periodicals. Having acquired the store from a longtime owner, the Culberts found it stocked with lots of items that he had never sold or gotten rid of, such as old-time medicine bottles.

"My dad was a pack rat," noted his son, Dan Culbert. "Seldom did he throw away anything of interest or value. One of the reasons the store is so priceless today is the boxes and boxes of every prescription that he ever filled in McGill. An anthropologist-historian would have a field day documenting the ills of the people of McGill over several decades."

Gerald died in 1979, and Elsa couldn't bring herself to sell the place. And she found she couldn't run it herself. So she locked it up, put out the CLOSED sign, and allowed it to sit there, fully stocked with magazines, books, toothpaste, and other items. Finally, in 1995 the Culbert children donated the drugstore—including inventory that dated back to the 1940s, original wooden display cases, and a soda fountain built in the 1930s—to the White Pine Public Museum for preservation and display. These days, visitors can tour this fully intact, mid-twentieth-century, small-town drugstore, which still has an operating soda fountain. The museum is open by appointment (775-235-7082).

Everyone will soon know your name if you stop into the legendary McGill Club.

photos of the hundreds of local boys who have served in the military, including many dating to World War II.

In addition to the impressive back-bar, which was built in 1910 and transported to McGill via ship, train, and wagon, the club's most valuable assets have been its bartenders, such as Norm Linnell, who poured drinks there for more than seventy years. Born in McGill in 1922, he began working in the club when he was fifteen years old. Although other barkeeps haven't been there quite as long, they all seem to have picked up his gift for sharing good-natured jokes and stories about local history.

Of course, part of the charm of the McGill Club is that, much like the town of McGill, nothing seems to change. A few decades ago, there might have been a few more open businesses in the town, but overall it wouldn't appear much different from how it looks now. Perhaps part of the reason is that McGill, located 12 miles north of Ely via U.S. Highway 93, was a company town. For decades nearly everyone who lived there worked for the Kennecott Copper Corporation. Founded in 1906, McGill was first a tent city that rose in the flats near the spot where the mining company built a massive smelter.

The unusually long life of the Ruth/Ely area's copper mines contributed to McGill's longevity. For much of the next fifty years, McGill maintained a relatively steady population of about 2,000 people, most of whom worked for the smelter. During its more than seventy-year mining boom, McGill acquired the amenities of a community, including churches, a newspaper, a movie theater, a large brick school, and a municipal swimming pool—actually an Olympic-size, old-fashioned watering hole. As a result of the mining company's aggressive recruitment of new immigrants, McGill also became one of Nevada's most ethnically diverse communities. Large numbers of Greeks, Irish, Slavs, and other newcomers to America found their way to McGill to work at the smelter.

But, as with all mining towns, when the mines closed, the jobs disappeared. In this case, it occurred in the early 1980s when Kennecott closed its eastern Nevada operations. Much of the town's population began to drift away during the 1980s. Construction of a state prison in the late 1980s did bring an influx of new people to McGill but not enough to change it. In 1993 Kennecott cleared away the remains of the old smelter complex, including the giant smokestack.

But that's just about the only thing that's changed much in McGill in the last century.

Nevada's Clay Cathedral

Panaca

In a state where the forces of nature have created some fairly weird stuff, Cathedral Gorge rates a mention. Located a few miles north of

The famous churches of the world have nothin' on Cathedral Gorge.

the Mormon farming community of Panaca, the gorge is a labyrinth of tall, deeply grooved, tan-brown, bentonite clay spires and cliffs with a definite gothic vibe. To understand how it was created, turn the geologic clock back about a million years to a time when much of this part of the state was underwater. Natural streams flowed into a large inland lake that covered the entire valley where the gorge is located today. Those streams also brought silt and clay that, over time, eventually filled the lake. Move ahead a few hundred thousand years, and the lake has dried up and left behind a thick, clay lake bed. Over time, wind and rain eroded the clay, forming it into the evocative shapes found in the gorge today.

The gorge contains several interesting self-guided hikes, which are marked. Two trails lead from the park and picnic area at the end

Pahranagat Valley's Peripatetic Pebbles

The Pahranagat Valley is a long, narrow patch of brown Nevada desert intersected by a ribbon of vegetation. This natural greenbelt, which parallels US 93 and runs down the center of the valley, is the result of two spring-fed finger lakes that stretch nearly the length of the valley—the Upper Pahranagat and the Lower Pahranagat. But, interestingly, it wasn't the valley's scenic lakes, which are now part of a national wildlife refuge, that first attracted attention to the area. It was the valley's rocks and boulders, which were said to have a mysterious power.

In the late nineteenth century, the Pahranagat Valley became the unlikely setting for one of nineteenth-century Nevada's most famous hoaxes. The perpetrator was veteran Virginia City journalist William Wright, who wrote under the pen name Dan De Quille. Like many of his contemporaries, including Mark Twain, Wright often crafted news stories that weren't always grounded in fact.

In 1867 Wright penned a tale about a man from the remote Pahranagat Valley who brought to Wright half a dozen round rocks that he described as "rolling stones." The man said that when spread apart, the rocks would mysteriously move back together. Wright wrote that the man could set the stones on the floor or table in a circle and they would immediately begin rolling toward one another in the center. In his story the journalist hypothesized that they did this because they were mostly made of magnetic lodestone or iron ore.

The story of the magical rolling rocks first appeared in Virginia City's *Territorial Enterprise* and was reprinted in papers throughout the country. Wright received hundreds of letters from curious readers, including the great showman P. T. Barnum, who wrote to offer $10,000 if Wright or anyone else could persuade the mobile rocks to perform

Photo courtesy of the Nevada Commission on Tourism

Pahranagat Valley was once the subject of a hoax involving self-animated boulders.

in his famous circus show. The tale continued to be told for more than a decade, and each time a whole new group of people wanted to see the amazing stones. Finally, in 1879, Wright decided that the con had gone on long enough. He wrote a brief news article debunking the story of the moving stones and revealing his part in the deception. Some, however, were skeptical about his retraction and believed he was lying so that he could keep the ambulatory agates for himself.

Still, if you happen to find yourself driving the length of the Pahranagat Valley, located about two hours northeast of Las Vegas via US 93, pull over to the side of the road and take a long, hard look at the rocks. If any move, grab 'em. Ringling Brothers is waiting.

of the paved entrance road to places called Moon Cave and Canyon Cave. Not really caves, both are narrow passages that wind through the dramatic clay walls. A 1-mile main trail leads into the center of the largest section of clay formations. Back in there, far from the parking lot and picnic tables, and deep inside the cool clay, you feel as though you've been transported to another world. At the end of the trail, you can climb a set of wooden steps that lead to the northern entrance to the park and a covered observation area known as the Miller's Point Overlook. From the overlook you can see almost the entire valley and admire the acres of marvelous clay sculptures.

The Nevada Division of State Parks has an attractive visitor center at Cathedral Gorge that provides information about all of the state parks in eastern Nevada. The center includes a small theater that shows videos describing Cathedral Gorge and the five other state parks in the region. Cathedral Gorge State Park (775-687-4370) is open throughout the year. The park has sixteen developed campsites with shaded picnic tables, an RV dump station, toilets, and showers; the campsites are open during the summer and fall. The best time of year to visit is in the spring, particularly following a wet March or April, when wildflowers bloom throughout the gorge.

Creative Financing

Pioche

Las Vegas didn't invent the skim or the kickback in Nevada. Both of these less than noble ways of doing business have been around for a long time—just ask the people of Pioche. In 1871 Pioche, located about three and a half hours north of Las Vegas via I-15 and US 93, was an up-and-coming mining town that had a reputation for lawlessness. In fact, it was reported that some seventy-two men were buried in the cemetery before anyone actually died of natural causes. Seeing the need for some kind of justice, the town snagged the Lincoln county seat away from the tinier community of Hiko and decided to build a solid, sturdy courthouse in which to hold trials and lock up

Pioche's Million Dollar Courthouse cost local residents a pretty penny.

its outlaws and badmen. The project was originally budgeted to cost $16,400, but a year later, when the two-story stone structure was completed, the price had skyrocketed to about $88,000 because of cost overruns, money skimmed off the top, and kickbacks to suppliers.

Unfortunately for Pioche, this huge bill arrived just as the town of about 7,000 residents was entering a mining slump. The county was unable to pay for the building, so it did what governments usually do in such situations—it made minimal payments and borrowed more money. When those bonds came due, the county still was unable to pay off the debt, so it refinanced the project, taking on additional interest. By the 1880s it's estimated that the amount due on the courthouse had risen to about $181,000, and the county just kept refinancing the debt. By the end of the century, Lincoln County owed more than $670,000 for its hall of justice. In fact, when the bill was finally paid in 1937, the county had paid nearly $1 million for the courthouse, which is why it's called Pioche's "Million Dollar Courthouse." Ironically, in 1933 the building was condemned and was replaced in 1937 by a new courthouse, which was paid off on schedule and remains in use. Despite its scandalous past, Pioche citizens took pride in their overpriced court building and made efforts to preserve it. In recent years the building has been renovated—for considerably less than a million dollars—and reopened as a museum and art gallery (www.lincolncountynevada.com). It is also used for community meetings and occasional theatrical performances.

Pioche's Lost Paintings

Pioche

In about 1870 Englishman Robert G. Schofield arrived in the mining town of Pioche. Jim McCormick, professor of art emeritus at the University of Nevada–Reno, describes Schofield as "a Renaissance man of sorts": Schofield was a gifted watchmaker, jeweler, engraver, house painter, and sign maker. He also penned poetry and offered lessons in drawing and French. And, between 1878 and 1913, he painted watercolors depicting the landscape and mining camps of eastern Nevada. McCormick, who has studied Schofield's work, notes that the artist used art paper that was rarely larger than the size of a piece of typing paper and painted with "short, almost fussy" brushstrokes that seemed to echo the work of the French impressionists. Colors were subdued and muted rather than bold and bright; McCormick says that Schofield may have used this color palette because of the limited range of pigments available at the time.

What makes the story of Schofield's paintings remarkable, however, is that he apparently painted them for his own pleasure—their existence wasn't known until they were rediscovered in 1950 by

Vern and Mary Smith. The Smiths bought Schofield's former home on Hoffman Street in Pioche. While cleaning out an old shed, the Smiths discovered a stack of old papers and documents, a box of tarnished silverware, and twenty-eight Schofield watercolors. Believing they were special, Mary Smith stored them away, occasionally showing them to friends and acquaintances. In the 1980s the Nevada Historical Society learned of their existence and helped to have them photographed and preserved. The paintings were eventually donated to the Lincoln County Historical Museum, which loaned them in 2000 to the Nevada Historical Society in Reno for an exhibition. These days, the watercolors can be seen in a gallery at the "Million Dollar Courthouse" in Pioche. The courthouse gallery (775-962-5182) is located on Main Street, at the north end of Pioche. It is open from 10:00 a.m. to 4:00 p.m., April through October.

The Truth Is Out There

Rachel

Perhaps no place in Nevada has captured the public's imagination as much as Area 51, also known as Dreamland or Groom Lake. Technically part of the Nevada Test Site, a 1,372-square-mile patch of desert where the nation has long tested its nuclear weapons, Area 51 is shrouded in mystery. Though generally recognized as being a super-secret military airbase, it has also long been linked with more extraterrestrial rumors, particularly involving so-called unidentified flying objects (UFOs). According to the Web-based encyclopedia *Wikipedia,* Area 51 "is not a conventional airbase. . . . It instead appears to be used during the development, testing, and training phases for new aircraft." The Web site, however, adds that because the base is so secure, it is reportedly also home to a small number of Soviet-designed aircraft, which apparently are analyzed there and used for training exercises.

It is known that during the 1950s Area 51 was the location used to test the U-2 spy plane and later for developing the SR-71 Blackbird,

Photo courtesy of the Nevada Commission on Tourism

The ET Highway skirts Area 51, America's favorite alien conspiracy site.

a high-speed reconnaissance airplane. Starting in the late 1970s, the military used the base for testing the prototypes for various "stealth" aircraft (planes that use technology that makes them undetectable), including precursors to the F-117 stealth fighter. In recent years rumors have surfaced of continued work on the next generation of military airplanes as well as stealth versions of cruise missiles, a stealthy vertical-take-off-and-landing (VTOL) transport craft, the "Aurora" supersonic spy plane, a stealth blimp, and a plane capable of flying in and out of space.

Some believe that the UFO sightings and stories are linked to the base's secretive operations and that the purported UFOs are merely the various high-tech planes that have been tested there. But others claim that Area 51 has underground facilities that house such things as spaceships from other planets and the bodies of alien creatures. This notion has been advanced in the popular media, including video games, fiction books, films such as *Independence Day,* and the TV show *The X-Files*. One popular theory is that Area 51 is where the U.S. government stored the flying saucer that allegedly crashed in Roswell, New Mexico, in the late 1940s.

Because of all the attention the area has received, in 1996 Nevada state tourism officials renamed the stretch of Route 375, which skirts the eastern edge of Area 51, as the official "Extraterrestrial Highway." The tiny town of Rachel (population: about 100), which sits on the highway, has taken to promoting itself as the official home of Area 51. A local business, The Little A'le'Inn, has a concrete time capsule it received from the production crew of the movie *Independence Day.* It serves up such fare as an "Alien" burger with secretions (cheese) and the Beam Me Up Scotty, a stiff whiskey drink designed to have you talking to any aliens in the bar. The diner also has a small library of UFO-related books as well as a gallery of grainy photos of alleged spaceships.

Over the past decade UFO aficionados have flocked to Rachel to try to catch a glimpse of something otherworldly. For a while, there were stories of a mysterious black mailbox, located a few miles from Rachel, that was allegedly for Area 51—as if the military would trust the mail for its top-secret base to a remote, unsecured mailbox on a lonely state highway. The truth was that the box belonged to a local rancher, who often found tourists rummaging through his mail hunting for secret documents. In 1996 he auctioned the famous black mailbox to a UFO fan—for $1,000!—and put up a new bulletproof, locking white mailbox to keep out the curious. Despite his efforts, some believe the removal of the black mailbox was part of a conspiracy, and others have covered the new mailbox with UFO-related graffiti. Go figure.

CHAPTER

4

Southwest

The Silver Trails

"There's not a fresh green vegetable in all of southwest Nevada. The state bird of Nevada is the chicken-fried steak. . . . The Nevada state song is the exaggerated belch."

—Tom Robbins, *Wild Ducks Flying Backward* (2005)

Perhaps it's true *that the farther you get from civilization, the more normal the abnormal can seem. Southwest Nevada—the portion of the state about equidistant from the Las Vegas and Reno urban areas—is a place where both Howard Hughes and Charlie Manson went to get lost. The region's thousands of square miles encompass not only the skeletons of bankrupt and defunct mining towns but also the Nevada test site, where America plays with its nuclear weapons. It's home to places with names like Death Valley, Devil's Hole, and Dead Horse Wells as well as the more optimistic Last Chance Creek.*

Southwest Nevada is the heart of the state's early-twentieth-century mining boom, in towns like Tonopah, Goldfield, and Rhyolite. Perhaps because of its mining roots—and recognizing that miners are the biggest dreamers of all—it is a part of the state where the improbable seems like it just might be possible. If some guy says he picked up one of the world's richest men passed out by the side of a dirt road in the middle of nowhere, it seems believable. If another guy wants to buy a ghost town and dress up as the town sheriff, it's all right. Out here, the state motto could be "anything goes."

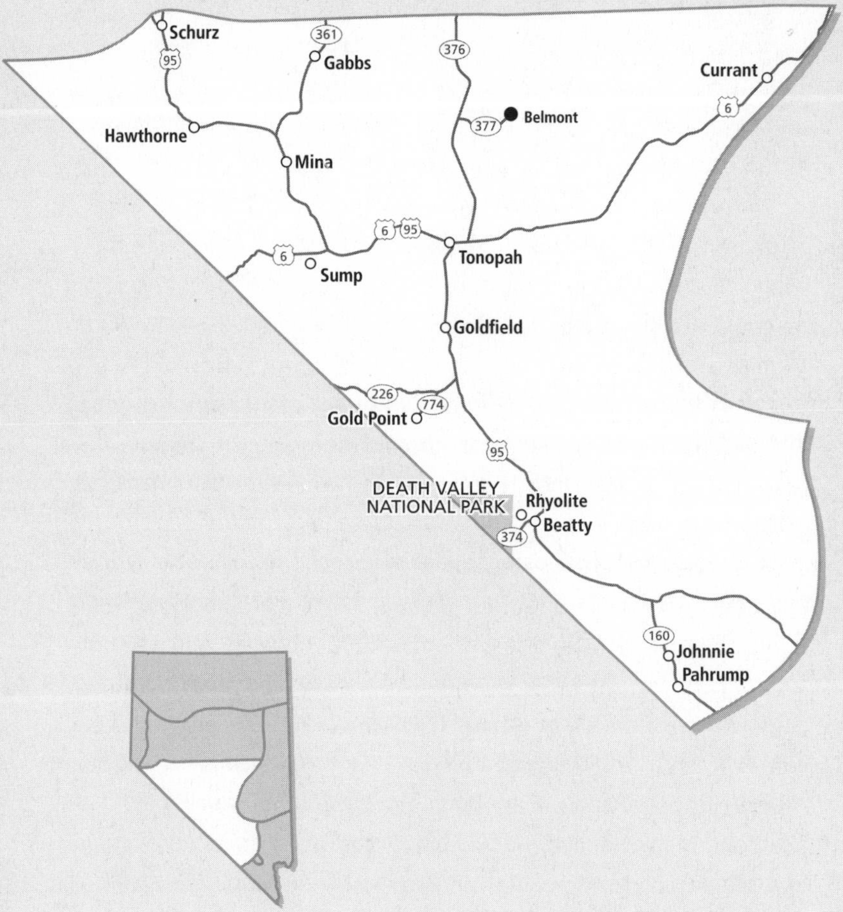
Schurz
95
361
Gabbs
376
Currant
6
377
Belmont
Hawthorne
Mina
6
95
Tonopah
6
Sump
Goldfield
226
774
Gold Point
95
DEATH VALLEY
NATIONAL PARK
Rhyolite
Beatty
374
160
Johnnie
Pahrump

Southwest

The True Story of Melvin and Howard

Beatty

To this day, Melvin Dummar insists that he met Howard Hughes on a cold December night in 1967. Dummar was driving on U.S. Highway 95, from his home in Gabbs, Nevada, to Los Angeles, when he pulled over to take a leak. On a lonely two-lane dirt road, he spotted a frail, bearded old man lying by the side of the road. Dummar stopped to check on the man's condition and found, to his relief, that the man was alive, albeit a little delirious. He helped the shivering old man into his car and agreed to take him to Las Vegas.

Warmed by the car heater, the man listened as Dummar sang a few songs and talked about how he had once tried to get a job at the Hughes Aircraft Company. The old man perked up and said he could get him a job at Hughes Aircraft because he was Howard Hughes and he owned the company. Dummar was amused but certain the old man was merely a bum who had spent too much time in the desert. Once in Las Vegas, the old man directed Dummar to drop him off at the Sands Hotel, where Hughes lived during the late 1960s.

Flash forward a few years, and the eccentric Hughes has died. A will has mysteriously surfaced in Salt Lake City that, among other things, names Dummar as a one-sixteenth beneficiary of the Hughes fortune. The will, however, was never formally filed, and its authenticity was immediately questioned. Following legal challenges, the will—known as the Mormon Will because it also included the Church of Jesus Christ of Latter-Day Saints as a beneficiary—was ruled a fake, and many claimed that Dummar concocted the whole scheme. In 1980 an Academy Award–winning movie, *Melvin and Howard,* was made based on the story. Dummar spent much of the money he received from the movie rights defending his story in court.

In 2005 Dummar was once again thrust into the public spotlight after the publication of a book written by a former FBI agent seemed to verify his story. Retired FBI agent Gary Magnesen wrote that

It was on a lonely stretch of US 95 near Beatty—like this one—that Melvin Dummar stumbled on Howard Hughes.

records and witnesses indicate that Hughes was in remote central Nevada at that time. A former Hughes pilot claims to have flown the industrialist to a brothel about 6 miles north of where he was picked up by Dummar, which would explain why Hughes wasn't wearing a coat or jacket. As a result of the new evidence, in June 2006 Dummar filed a lawsuit that again asked for his share of the Hughes will (about $156 million). A year later, however, a Utah judge tossed out the suit.

These days, Dummar, who lives in northern Utah, drives a frozen-meat truck and continues to insist that he really did meet Howard Hughes on that December night in the desert.

Charlie Manson Nearly Slept Here

Belmont

In 1969 cult leader Charles Manson and his followers were on the lam in Nevada. In mid-August several members of his sect had brutally murdered actress Sharon Tate (wife of director Roman Polanski) as well as three of her friends. The group was also responsible for killing at least three other people, including a wealthy businessman named Leno LaBianca and his wife, Rosemary. Manson believed that committing the heinous crimes, which included political statements written in the victims' blood, would spark a race war.

In the months following the murders, Manson and his family, as his small group of followers was known, lived in a number of remote desert sites, including the Barker Ranch, a dilapidated homestead in the Goler Wash, now part of Death Valley National Park. Reportedly, he believed that he and his followers could hide in the desert and wait out the great race war that would erupt following the murders. During this period the group also wandered into the central Nevada ghost town of Belmont. According to one account, when Manson and his family members arrived in Belmont, they were greeted by Rose Walter, a lifelong resident of the old town, who lived in one of the few maintained buildings in the community (her house is now the site of the Monitor Inn, a bed-and-breakfast).

Walter was accustomed to strangers appearing in the ghost town to explore the surroundings and take photos of the abandoned, decaying structures, many of which were nearly a century old. She is said to have invited the half dozen or so young people to explore all they wanted but reminded them that overnight camping was prohibited. Reportedly, she thought the group looked a little scruffy, like many of the hippies of the day, but they were well mannered and respectful.

Manson and his clan wandered Belmont for several hours, even spending time inside the abandoned Belmont Courthouse, originally built in 1865. While there, Manson carved his initials into the court-

Inside the historic remains of the old Belmont Courthouse are carved the initials of cult leader Charles Manson.

house wall. Eventually, Manson and family decided to depart. About a month later, Walter was visiting some friends when she saw a TV report about the trial of Manson and several of his followers for the Tate-LaBianca murders. Walter recognized the long-haired, bearded young man with the intense eyes as the driver of the van that had stopped in Belmont a few weeks earlier. For years after, she enjoyed sharing her story of her brush with the infamous Charles Manson but wondered what might have happened had her encounter gone another way.

And, yes, Manson's initials can still be seen, carved into the courthouse wall.

Pupfish's Distinction May Be Extinction

Death Valley National Park

One of the most endangered species on the planet is the Devil's Hole pupfish, an inch-long, iridescent blue fish found only in a warm spring-fed crevice in a corner of Death Valley National Park that is known as Devil's Hole. Today, less than forty of the fish are believed to exist in their natural habitat. The story of what happened to this imperiled species is one filled with miscalculations and mistakes. Scientists first noticed the Devil's Hole fish in 1890 but didn't recognize that it was a distinct and separate type of pupfish until 1930. In 1952 the little creature was given formal protection after Devil's Hole was

Ash Meadows is home of Devil's Hole, last refuge of the endangered Devil's Hole pupfish, as well as several other natural springs with their own rare pupfish, such as Crystal Springs.

made part of Death Valley National Monument. Subsequent studies of the fish resulted in its being named an endangered species in 1967.

The Devil's Hole pupfish is believed to have been around for at least 22,000 years. Its habitat is extremely precarious; the fish only seem to thrive just below the surface of the 93-degree water in Devil's Hole, in the area above a shallow, submerged limestone shelf that is only a few feet wide. This tiny ecosystem is the only natural place where the fish can spawn and feed.

Of course, the pupfish's environment is easily affected by external factors such as earthquakes and flash floods, which can raise or lower the chasm's water level and threaten the survival of the species. Moreover, in the 1970s the pumping of groundwater for agricultural reasons in the surrounding valley began to lower the water level in Devil's Hole, causing a radical drop in the number of pupfish. This led to a landmark 1976 Supreme Court decision in favor of the fish and restricting groundwater pumping in the valley.

To encourage the survival of the species, federal wildlife officials transported a small number of the pupfish to temperature-controlled concrete tanks at Hoover Dam and established two additional colonies in artificial habitats at Ash Meadows in the 1980s and 1990s. Ironically, the scientific efforts to monitor the fish nearly led to the demise of the entire population. In 2004 an estimated sixty cubic feet of dirt and debris, including fish traps and other equipment placed around Devil's Hole to keep track of the creatures, was swept into the hole during a flash flood. As a result, about half of the pupfish population was killed. Then, in 2006, wildlife experts discovered that an invasive species of snails had somehow infested the Hoover Dam tank, causing officials to remove all of the adult fish to other facilities, including the Shark Reef aquarium inside the Mandalay Bay Resort in Las Vegas.

As of 2007 an estimated thirty-eight pupfish still live in Devil's Hole and another twenty-nine in other places. Many experts believe that the species may already have dropped below the numbers needed to keep the population viable.

Nevada's Second-Oldest Saloon

Goldfield

Nevada saloons often like to brag about being the first or the oldest or the longest operating. Inevitably, some myth-busting historian or a rival bar owner comes along and challenges such claims. So the Santa Fe Saloon in Goldfield (925 North Fifth Street; 775-485-3431) decided to sidestep the issue. It calls itself the "second-oldest saloon in continuous operation" in the state—just about as convoluted a boast as anyone will ever make. According to a few locals, the Santa Fe purposely decided to be the second oldest because nobody ever argues about being number two.

Although it's possible that the claim isn't true, it is a fact that the Santa Fe Saloon has been around for more than a century. The worn wooden shack of a saloon opened in 1905 and has been operating, as far as anyone can tell, since then (although it's unclear whether it remained quietly open during Prohibition). Unlike many of Goldfield's businesses, the saloon isn't located in the center of the community but rather sits at the entrance to the area's once-thriving mining district. It's one of two watering holes in Goldfield; the other is the Mozart Club, which also is the only restaurant in town.

Inside, the Santa Fe Saloon exudes an old-time ambience with its uneven floors, low ceilings, impressive oak back-bar, and, seated at a rickety table, a mannequin dressed as an Indian, which serves as a sort of saloon mascot. The latter appears in just about every photograph ever taken of the bar's interior. The Santa Fe Saloon has the only overnight accommodations in Goldfield, offering four motel rooms (built in the 1990s, so they're not original). The front of the saloon building has a weathered-wood front porch and sidewalks, as well as one of those old-fashioned frontier facades upon which the bar's name is painted. A local acting troupe that specializes in mock gunfights makes regular appearances to rile up the tourists.

No Spitting Allowed

Goldfield

There's a sign in the hallway outside the courtroom in the Esmeralda County Courthouse stating, GENTLEMEN WILL NOT EXPECTORATE IN THE HALLWAY. Inside, the courtroom, which originally cost $125,000, boasts original Tiffany stained-glass lamps and high-end frontier accents, like brass gaslight fixtures and wire loops underneath the wooden courtroom seats where a visitor can safely stow his or her cowboy hat. It's a classy hall of justice.

Built in 1907–1908, the imposing stone courthouse hints at Goldfield's past grandeur. Gold—hence the name—was discovered there in 1902, and within a few years the community had ballooned into Nevada's largest city, with about 20,000 residents. The ore, however, was about a mile wide and an inch deep. After about a decade of

Photo courtesy of the Nevada Commission on Tourism

The elegant Esmeralda County Courthouse in Goldfield boasts Tiffany lamps, brass fixtures, and a "no spitting" sign.

prosperity, Goldfield's boom was over, and the population quickly drifted off.

But unlike many Nevada mining towns, Goldfield never completely faded away. The courthouse, which has remained in operation throughout the years, is one of the best-maintained buildings in Goldfield. The mission-revival structure has a dramatic, castlelike appearance that is created by its coarse stone exterior; a tall, stepped parapet at the roofline above the entrance; and notched walls at the four corners. Inside, it has finely crafted wood staircases, ornate light fixtures, and expensive courtroom furnishings, including those cool Tiffany lamps. If you want to see them, however, you'll have to ask a court employee to unlock the doors. A few years ago, one of the employees wandered into the room and caught a visitor trying to remove the lamps, which are attached to the judge's bench. The Esmeralda County Courthouse is located at 233 Crook Street (US 95) in Goldfield (about 185 miles north of Las Vegas).

The Sheriff of Gold Point

Gold Point

Herb Robbins loves ghost towns. In fact, he loves them so much that he bought most of one. Since the 1970s Robbins, a wallpaper hanger by trade, has been purchasing lots in the historic mining town of Gold Point, located about 25 miles southwest of Goldfield. Over the years he and his partners, Walt and Chuck Kremin, have bought more than a hundred lots, most with buildings on them. Their goal is to restore or preserve as many of the old buildings as they can so that they'll still be around for future generations to enjoy.

"We are not doing this for the money as we know we will never get out what we will have put into them," Robbins writes on his Web site (www.goldpointghosttown.com). "These buildings will be 100 years old in 2008. Each building we save we hope will see another 100 years. This will be our legacy."

In 1998 Robbins's efforts to save Gold Point were given a boost

Photo courtesy of the Nevada Commission on Tourism

A fine point: for years, Herb Robbins has been trying to restore the community of Gold Point.

when he won a $226,000 jackpot at a Las Vegas casino. Naturally, he poured nearly all of it into restoring the dilapidated wooden structures in his personal ghost town. The bearded Robbins, who often dresses in jeans, boots, and a cowboy hat (he calls his frontier persona Sheriff Harold T. Stone), discovered Gold Point in 1978, while on a ghost town pilgrimage with Chuck Kremin. The nearly abandoned town, which consisted of about fifty ramshackle buildings and one or two permanent residents, made an impression on them. A few months later, Robbins and Kremin learned of three lots for sale in Gold Point—and their dream of owning a piece of a ghost town soon became a reality.

"I wanted to say I owned a piece of a ghost town (so I purchased two of them)," he recalls. "They were $500 apiece, and just a bunch of sagebrush, but that kind of got us started."

Robbins began spending time in the ghost town, sleeping under the stars, soaking up the atmosphere, and imagining life in an early-twentieth-century mining camp. In 1981 the post office was put up for sale. He purchased it and subsequently bought other buildings. "It was a gradual thing that came upon me as I was fixing up some of the buildings. I got such a sense of gratitude that I was saving some part of American history . . . [and] we've just kept buying and buying."

These days, Robbins jokes, "I have to go hang wallpaper to support my habit out there." A few years ago, he did begin allowing ghost town enthusiasts to rent a night in one of a handful of mining cabins that he and his friends have restored. The accommodations are not luxurious, and they're available only on Saturday nights because of his work schedule, but Robbins, who lives in a restored cabin in the town, says that they do bring in a little extra money, which helps with his efforts to save the town. For reservations call Robbins at (775) 482-4653 or e-mail him at sheriffstone@goldpoint ghosttown.com.

Hawthorne's Exploding Mounds

Hawthorne

From the air, the town of Hawthorne looks as though giant earthen and grass-covered caterpillars surround it. More than 2,400 dirt and concrete humps spread out across the flat valley around this community of about 3,700 residents. These brown, oblong bunkers are filled with an estimated 300,000 tons of military ammunition, about half of which is so old that it is scheduled for disposal. The mounds, which cover some 147,000 acres, were specifically designed with steel-reinforced concrete blast walls to explode upward should there ever be an accidental detonation—which is exactly what happened in 1984 and again in the early 1990s, when bunkers did accidentally explode.

Surprisingly, most Hawthornians are pretty laid-back about the town's status as the place most likely to explode on the face of the earth. In fact, they embrace their heritage as the nation's bomb stockpile—one of the town's main attractions is the Hawthorne Ordnance Museum, a place that celebrates the area's four-decade history as a weapons storehouse. Located inside a former car dealership, the museum displays a variety of now-harmless weapons of mass destruction, including torpedoes, land mines, bombs, guns, and other former instruments of war.

The reason Hawthorne became America's munitions dump can be traced to a devastating explosion that occurred at the Naval Ammunition Depot at Lake Denmark, New Jersey, in 1927. The accident demolished the depot and an adjacent arsenal and severely damaged the surrounding communities. Twenty-one people died, and another fifty-three were seriously injured. After the disaster the U.S. government began looking around the country for a more remote, less heavily populated place in which to store the nation's ammo. A year later, a federal committee recommended that the railroad town of Hawthorne (population: about 500) be the site of the new facility. During World War II things were hopping in Hawthorne. The military employed more than 5,600 people at the depot, which became the staging area for bombs, rockets, and ammunition for the nation's war effort. As a result, Hawthorne boomed, achieving its peak population of about 13,000 in 1944.

But it's been a downhill slide ever since. Following the war, the government cut back on the number of employees and eventually outsourced the plant to a private firm. In 2005 a federal military-base-closure commission recommended shutting down the depot, which would have meant the loss of half of the town's jobs. Nevada's congressional delegation, however, successfully fought to keep it open.

If you want find out more about such stuff as how local residents can sleep soundly at night knowing they are surrounded by more than 300,000 tons of bombs, be sure to stop by the Ordnance Museum on the corner of Ninth and E Streets. It's open from 10 a.m. to 3:00 p.m. Monday through Saturday. Admission is free. For more information call (775) 945-5400.

Truly Local TV

Hawthorne

In a world where bigger is supposed to mean better, Channel 13 in the central Nevada town of Hawthorne proves that there are exceptions. TV13, which goes by the call letters KWI, is Nevada's smallest TV station. It broadcasts with a mighty 10 watts of power, which, according to writer Chuck Woodbury, is "enough to reach every person in Hawthorne and every fish in Walker Lake."

Founded in 1994, TV13 is an FCC-licensed television station that is housed in an old single-wide mobile home. It has a 50-foot tower, a single satellite dish to pick up its programming (it broadcasts religious shows and old network TV programs distributed by the American Life cable network), a used transmitter, and an assortment of vintage tape decks, VCRs, and microphones. TV13 is owned by Virginia and Bob Becker; the permit for the station was originally a Father's Day gift to Bob from his son, Scott, who owns a low-power TV station in Kansas. The couple cobbled together the necessary equipment for a TV station and started broadcasting.

TV13 covers some local events, like the Armed Forces Day Parade, the Walker Lake Loon Festival, the Miss Mineral County pageant, high school sports, and meetings of the Mineral County Commission. The station is largely supported by advertising, which consists mainly of ad messages crawling across the bottom of the screen during the various shows. Every once in a while, the station will break into its regular programming to broadcast tape of a breaking news story, such as the time a potato truck overturned on US 95.

Katie Couric has to be jealous.

Nevada's First Feminist

Mina

There weren't too many women on the Nevada frontier like Ferminia Sarras. Born in Nicaragua in 1840, Sarras and her husband arrived in the Silver State in the 1870s. Within a few years she had shed her husband and was prospecting in Belleville, near the central Nevada mining town of Candelaria. There, she made a small fortune, which she lost speculating on mining stocks and in other, less successful mining ventures. In 1895 she began mining in the mountains above Soda Spring Valley and staked a number of promising copper claims. Sarras sold about two dozen of these sites at a handsome profit.

Once she was flush with cash, she followed the lead of so many of her male counterparts—she spent it with reckless abandon. Sarras, who was sometimes known as "the Copper Queen," headed to San Francisco, rented a room at one of the city's most expensive hotels, went on a shopping spree to buy the most expensive garments, indulged in fine food and beverage, picked up a lover, and pampered herself until all her money was gone. Then she returned to the Nevada desert to do it all over again.

She was equally libertine in her personal life. It's believed that she married anywhere from three to six times and had countless lovers, usually men who were much younger. Her uncanny knack for finding productive claims provided her with a measure of local notoriety, and in the summer of 1905 the new railroad town of Mina, located southeast of Hawthorne, was named in her honor—one of the few towns in the state ever named after a woman. By the time she died in 1915, she had made—and lost—several fortunes. Some believe that before she died, she buried a fortune in gold coins in a chicken coop. Her stash has never been found.

Heidi's Stud Farm—and Laundromat

Pahrump

It was probably just a matter of time before the notorious former Hollywood madam Heidi Fleiss—who served nearly two years in prison for, among other things, pandering—discovered the benefits of living in the only state in the Union that allows legal prostitution. Fleiss made headlines in the 1990s after it was discovered that she ran a high-priced call girl ring for Hollywood stars and wealthy busi-

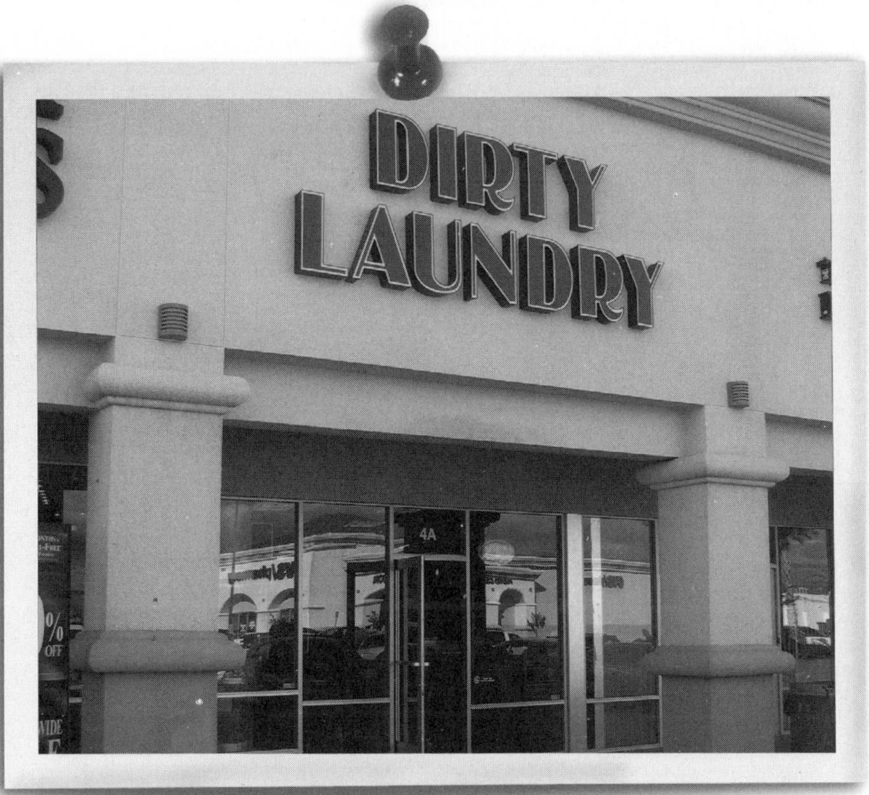

Proving there is life after Hollywood, former "Madam to the Stars" Heidi Fleiss opens Dirty Laundry, a laundromat in Pahrump.

nessmen. In December 2005 Fleiss moved from Beverly Hills to rural Pahrump, Nevada, located about 45 miles west of Las Vegas. Having sold the movie rights to her juicy past for a reported $5 million, Fleiss rented a house in Pahrump and purchased sixty acres in Crystal, about 20 miles north of Pahrump. On the latter site, she said she wanted to open Heidi's Stud Farm, a brothel that would cater exclusively to female customers.

Fleiss, who by late 2007 still had not submitted an application to Nye County officials to operate her male whorehouse, told *Las Vegas Review-Journal* reporter Henry Brean that she has been inundated with e-mails from men offering their services in her proposed brothel and claimed that she had "at least 400 women" ready to buy memberships. In the meantime, in July 2007 Fleiss opened a 1,000-square-foot Laundromat in Pahrump that she named Dirty Laundry. She said that she had sunk more than $200,000 into the business, located in the town's busiest strip mall. In addition to having thirteen coin-operated washers and fourteen dryers, the twenty-four-hour-a-day establishment boasts a vintage gambling decor, complete with displays of slot machine and video poker nameplates.

Fleiss said that in addition to overseeing the Laundromat, which has a five-year lease, she eventually wants to couple her brothel with a large-scale, commercial wind farm. Once she is able to get the wind farm going, she hopes to make enough money so that she'll never have to work again.

While you're waiting for her to open her other enterprises, you can check out Fleiss's Dirty Laundry, which is located in the Pahrump Valley Junction Shopping Center, 20 South Highway 160 in Pahrump. Inside, it looks just like a typical coin-operated Laundromat, albeit with cool gaming memorabilia on the walls. And after driving all that way, you might even decide to do a bit of laundry. Heidi might appreciate it.

Art Oasis

Rhyolite

In the early 1980s the late Belgian artist Charles Albert Szukalski discovered the beauty of the Nevada desert. A renowned sculptor and artist in Europe, he was drawn to the stark, open landscape. In 1984 he moved to Beatty, Nevada (located about 115 miles north of Las Vegas), and began working on *The Last Supper,* a surreal, life-size re-creation of Leonardo da Vinci's painting of the same name that features ghostly silhouettes of Jesus and his apostles made from white plaster and fiberglass. The artist recruited townspeople to pose in shrouds covered with hundreds of pounds of plaster. Szukalski said he created the work because the surroundings reminded him of Jesus' homeland in the Middle East.

Trivia

The Legend of the Lost Breyfogle Mine

Nearly every western state has its legends of lost treasure—and Nevada is no exception. Perhaps the most enduring of the Silver State's tales of wealth found and lost is the story of the Lost Breyfogle Mine. According to most versions of the legend, in 1863 prospector Charles Breyfogle was traveling with three other men in the Amargosa River Valley when hostile Indians attacked the group. The others were killed, but Breyfogle managed to escape with little more than his clothing and a bedroll. He wandered around in the desert for several days until he found a spring, where he stopped to hydrate and rest.

While filling his boots with water, he noticed gold in a quartz deposit. He chipped off several samples and vowed to return. He made his way south and stopped at a place called Stump Spring in the Pahrump Valley to wait for a wagon to show up. Unfortunately, another group of Indians came along and captured him. According to one account, he was forced to gather wood and perform other menial chores for the tribe during his enslavement. After a few months, however, Mormon travelers arrived at the Indian village and agreed to pay a ransom to free him. Breyfogle, who had somehow managed to hang on to his gold samples, was taken to a ranch at Manse Spring, near present-day Pahrump, where he regained his strength and shared the news of his discovery.

Breyfogle settled in the mining town of Austin, where he told others of his fabulous discovery and organized several expeditions to try to relocate the site of the spring filled with gold. For the next quarter

Not much remains of the mining camp near Death Valley, believed to be the location of the famous Lost Breyfogle Mine.

century, he wandered through the region northeast of Death Valley and in the vicinity of Beatty searching in vain for his lost stake. It is believed that he died in the late nineteenth century, still insisting that his gold discovery was real. According to some historians, a gold strike in 1891 in the Johnnie Mining District near Death Valley was the site of Breyfogle's discovery.

Others, however, believe that Breyfogle's gold is still out there waiting to be reclaimed.

The work, built on the top of a hill overlooking the ghost town of Rhyolite, was unveiled to little fanfare later that year. Within a short time, however, vandals had destroyed three of the figures, so Szukalski bought about eight acres on the edge of Rhyolite and relocated the figures to his property. He restored the work and added other sculptures, such as *Ghost Rider,* a shrouded ghost figure holding a bicycle, and *Desert Flower,* a twisted mass of shiny chrome sprouting from the ground. He also recruited other artist friends to join him in creating an outdoor art gallery on his property.

Art needs fresh air and sunshine, too, as evidenced by the Goldwell Open Air Museum.

Within a few years Szukalski's pieces had been joined by Andre (Dre) Peeters's *Icara,* a giant wooden sculpture based on the Greek myth about Icarus, and Fred Devoets's *Tribute to Shorty Harris,* a large metal outline of a prospector and a penguin. The latter is said to have been included because the artist felt out of place in the desert—just as a penguin would. In 1992 Dr. Hugo Heyrman added *Lady Desert: The Venus of Nevada,* a massive pink cinderblock representation of a woman (it looks like a huge Lego creation), while local artist, David Spicer, chipped in with *Chained to the Earth,* a stone monolith with holes that represents, in his words, "the inseparability of man and woman, and the need for humankind to come back to earth."

Following Szukalski's death in 2000, his outdoor sculpture garden and land were donated to a nonprofit organization, the Goldwell Open Air Museum (www.goldwellmuseum.org), to maintain the pieces and develop art programs. The museum is located about 4 miles west of Beatty, on the road leading to Rhyolite.

Bottoms Up

Rhyolite

The desert around the ghost town of Rhyolite is barren and dry. There are no trees and few shrubs. So, when it came to building materials, residents were forced to get creative—like saloon owner Tom Kelly, who built a three-room house using an estimated 30,000 used beer bottles, held together with adobe. According to the Friends of Rhyolite, a local preservation group, it took Kelly a little less than six months to construct the unusual home, which was completed in February 1906. The Adolphus Busch Company (today known as Budweiser) manufactured nearly all of the beer bottles, which apparently were acquired from the several dozen saloons that operated in the Rhyolite area. Based on the condition of some of the bottles, it's also known that Kelly didn't wash the bottles before using them.

Kelly, who was seventy-six years old when he built the house, abandoned it a few years later, most likely because the Rhyolite mining boom was over. In 1925 a movie studio, Paramount Pictures, discovered the nearly abandoned town of Rhyolite and the quaint bottle house, which was featured in a silent film, *The Air Mail,* which starred Warner Baxter, Billie Dove, and Douglas Fairbanks Jr. The studio is believed to have spruced up the house and possibly repaired its roof.

In the mid-1950s Tommy and Mary Thompson occupied the house with their children and opened it to the public as a museum and rock

The Rhyolite Bottle House is one of Nevada's earliest recycling projects.

shop. Following their deaths in the late 1960s, their son Evan maintained the property until about 1989.

In 1990 the Bureau of Land Management assumed responsibility for the structure, which was starting to require significant restoration. In the 1990s a large hole developed near the south gable, as the wall began to collapse. In 2005 the building underwent a significant reconstruction that included a new roof and shingles, bracing for the walls and roof, and reconstruction of the front porch. In addition, the glass-bottle walls were rebuilt to replace cracked or missing bottles, and new adobe was laid between the bottles.

These days, the bottle house is one of the best-looking structures in the ghost town. Volunteers throughout the year offer guided tours of the town. For more information go to www.rhyolitesite.com.

A Place That's Sumpin' Special

Sump

If the Sump had a cooler name, it might have been made into a state park or a national monument years ago. Hidden in a remote part of Southwest Nevada in some hills at the north end of the Fish Lake Valley, the Sump is a geologic wonderland of petrified wood stumps and mounds, solitary clay pillars, and colorful cliffs and hills. As for that name, the dictionary defines a sump as "a pit, cistern, or cesspool for draining liquid." Though technically an accurate description of the place, it doesn't exactly have the same ring as Valley of Fire or Devil's Hole.

The Sump, which sits on public lands, doesn't appear on many maps. The site is located near Fish Lake Valley off US 95 between Hawthorne and Tonopah. A high-clearance vehicle, preferably with four-wheel drive, is recommended. To reach the site, head south of Hawthorne on US 95 to Coaldale Junction. Drive west on U.S. Highway 6 for about 6 miles and then turn south on Route 773. Continue 9 miles before turning left on a dirt road. If you reach the intersection

Trivia

Wovoka and the Ghost Dance

There's a grave in the Paiute Cemetery in the town of Schurz (located about 100 miles southeast of Reno) with a headstone much larger than those around it. It's the grave of Jack Wilson, also known as Wovoka, the Paiute Messiah. In the late nineteenth century, Wovoka was the leader of a Native American religious movement, known as the Ghost Dance, which, for a time, swept the Indian nation.

The Ghost Dance encouraged its followers to be good to others, to cease hostilities with whites, and not to steal. By doing those things and regularly engaging in a frenzied, five-day dancing ritual, participants would go to a place with no sickness, death, or disease to be reunited with ancestors and loved ones who had died. The religion borrowed aspects of previous Native American religious movements as well as elements of Christian beliefs.

Wovoka was born near Yerington, Nevada, in 1856. In 1887 he had a vision that told him how to help the Indian people achieve a happy afterlife. He began preaching to local tribes, and word of his new religion spread. However, the movement evolved as it moved farther away from the source. Soon, some followers proclaimed that the dance would make all the whites disappear, and others began wearing "Ghost Shirts," which were thought to make the wearer bulletproof.

The movement came to a tragic end at Wounded Knee in December 1890 when U.S. Army troops opened fire on a crowd of Lakota Sioux who were participating in the Ghost Dance. The soldiers launched the assault because they believed that the Sioux were preparing to

Paiute Messiah Wovoka sparked the Ghost Dance Indian religious movement.

attack them. When the shooting ended, the great chief Sitting Bull had been killed along with 150 Sioux, mostly women and children. The massacre hastened the end of the Ghost Dance movement, although Wovoka continued to be a revered spiritual leader for the rest of his life. He died in Yerington in 1932.

The Sump is an oddly named geological site formed when a prehistoric lake drained and left behind unusual clay and rock formations.

of Routes 773 and 264, you've gone about 0.4 mile too far. Proceed about 0.5 mile on the dirt road to a wide wash. You can park and walk from here, or you can carefully drive into the wash (there is a steep drop), which is sandy in places. Turn left and continue about 1.5 miles to the lower end of the Sump.

Should you make the trek, you'll find an amazing 1.5-mile-long gorge filled with tall, twisted clay and rock columns, smooth mounds, and rippled cliff walls that resemble folded curtains. The name Sump is derived from the fact that the canyon is a natural wash that drains into the surrounding flats.

In geologic terms, the Sump formed some twenty-five million years ago. At that time, the entire area was submerged beneath a large lake, now called Lake Esmeralda. Over millions of years, sediment was carried into the lake by streams and creeks. Eventually, the mud built up and hardened while the lake disappeared. Later, major geologic forces uplifted the area and created the mountain ranges around the Sump. During the past few thousand years, erosion has worn down the sediment and carved out the gorge. The wind and rain have also exposed the multicolored layers of soil as well as shaped the area's unusual towers and pillars. Furthermore, the Sump contains the remnants of a grove of petrified trees. In most cases, the tree stumps stand on mounds of solidified mud, surrounded by countless brown chips. From a distance the mounds actually look like piles of wood chips.

Now if only someone could come up with a better name.

CHAPTER

5

Central
Nevada's Outback

"Highway 50 cuts through what Nevada natives like to call Real Nevada. In Real Nevada, the range is still open, the air is pure, and the cattle graze right out on the highway."
—James Lilliefors, *Highway 50: Ain't That America!* (1993)

Over the decades *U.S. Highway 50 through central Nevada has been called a lot of things: the Loneliest Road in America, the Lincoln Highway, the Jackass Mail, the Pony Express, the Overland Stage Route. Some have said that it's completely empty and has no points of interest, whereas others have described it as a "multi-million year old Nature Park built by colliding plates and stretching continent."*

The terrain defines this part of Nevada. Across the state's midriff are dozens of north-south mountain ranges interrupted by wide, dry valleys.

US 50 winds over and around these ranges for some 400 miles between California and Utah. It includes old mining towns, such as Austin, Eureka, and Ely, as well as agricultural centers like Fallon. It passes natural wonders, like Sand Mountain; man-made oddities, such as the Old Shoe Tree; and things that are a combination of the two, such as Soda Lake.

Perhaps central Nevada is the real Nevada.

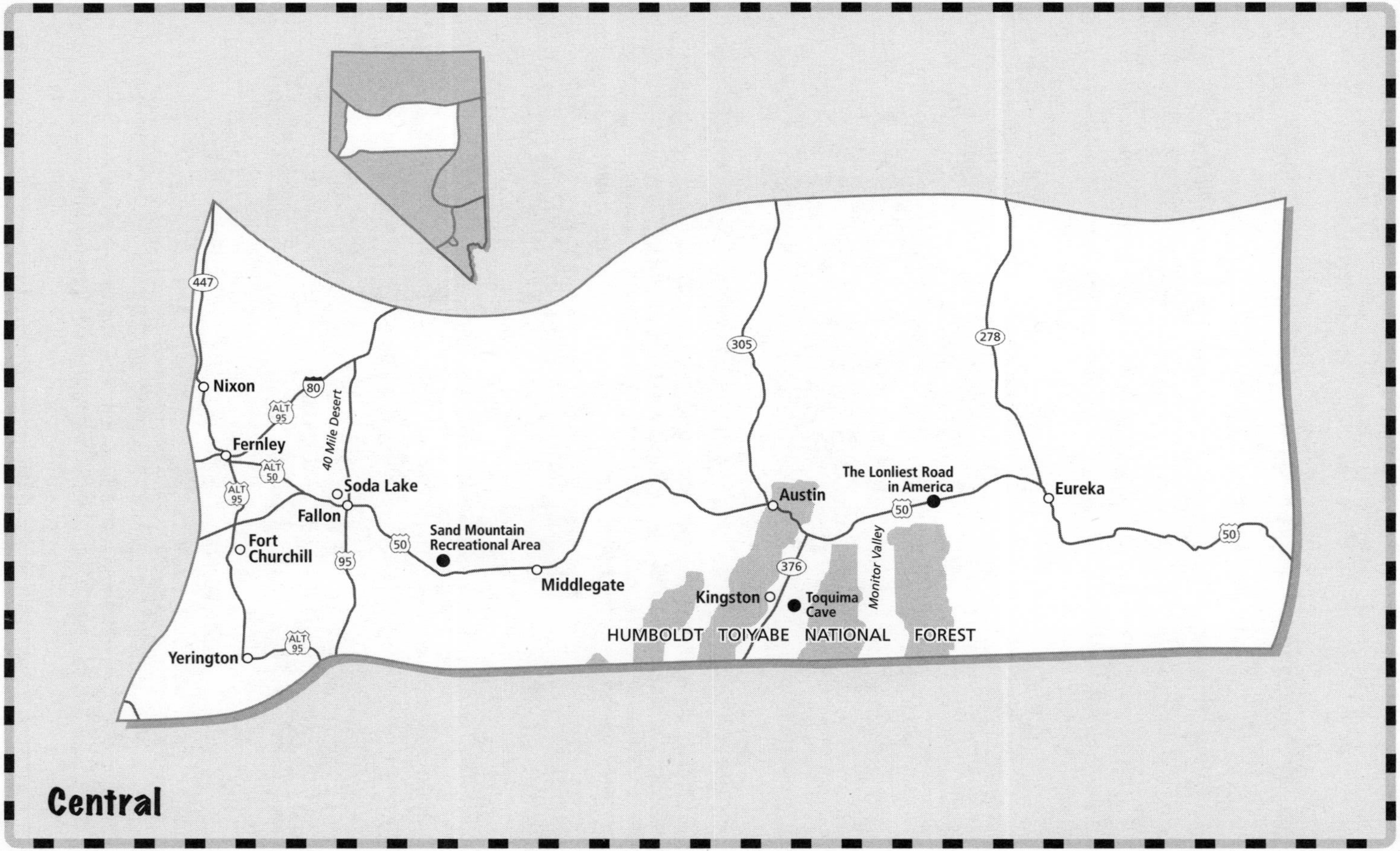
Central
Nixon
Fernley
40 Mile Desert
Soda Lake
Fallon
Fort Churchill
Yerington
Sand Mountain Recreational Area
Middlegate
Austin
Kingston
Toquima Cave
Monitor Valley
The Lonliest Road in America
Eureka
HUMBOLDT TOIYABE NATIONAL FOREST
447
80
ALT 95
ALT 50
50
95
305
376
278

Mr. Stokes's Summer Cottage

Austin

Anson Phelps Stokes was so rich that in 1896, when he decided to build a little summerhouse for his sons so that they could keep an eye on his mining and railroad properties in Austin, Nevada, he opted for something grand and unusual—he wanted a stone castle that resem-

The original McMansion: Stokes Castle is a strange house built by a rich guy who hardly lived in it.

bled a Roman villa he had seen outside Rome. The seasonal home, known today as Stokes Castle, was unlike anything else in Austin. Built on the west side of the Toiyabe Range, about a mile from Austin, it rose three stories high and was built of slabs of native granite held in position by wedging and clay mortar. Wooden balconies surrounded the second and third stories, and each floor had a fireplace. The first floor contained the kitchen and dining room (the place had indoor plumbing), while the second level served as the living room. The top floor had two bedrooms, and the roof was a battlemented terrace with an open-air viewing area that offered spectacular views of the Reese River Valley (reportedly, one could see 60 miles to the south and 35 miles to the north).

After the structure was completed in 1897, the family lived in it for about a month in June and July of that year. But money was not in short supply for the Stokes family. A member of one of America's wealthiest families, Stokes had made a fortune in banking before becoming involved in mining in Nevada. In the 1870s he financed construction of the Nevada Central Railroad, which ran from Austin to Battle Mountain. In the late nineteenth century, he built a grand estate called Shadowbrook in Massachusetts, which at the time was the largest private residence ever built in the United States.

After the summer of 1897, the family never returned to the fully furnished castle, which fell into disrepair. Eventually, the balconies collapsed—you can still see the metal supports projecting out of the structure's exterior walls—as did the interior floors and roof. For many years local kids would climb inside the building to scratch or write their names and initials into the stucco-over-stone walls. A few decades ago, a fence was erected around the tall, rectangular stone landmark, which is privately owned, and a historic marker was installed adjacent to the tower to explain its story. A narrow dirt road about 0.5 mile west of Austin leads from US 50 to the site.

The Many Tales of Austin's Churches

Austin

In the 1860s and 1870s, the mining town of Austin, located about 180 miles east of Reno via US 50, was home to about 6,000 souls and boasted many of the finest churches in the state. Although the town has fallen on hard times—there has been little serious mining in decades—three classic houses of worship have survived.

The Methodist Church, built in 1866, was once the largest building in town. Built in the Gothic revival style, the church was financed in an unusual way. The local minister, Reverend Trefren, formed a business corporation, which he named the Methodist Mining Company, to raise funds. The company's assets included mining stock certificates that had been donated to the church. Reverend Trefren traveled to his home state of New Hampshire, where he sold more than $250,000 in his company's stock. His sales pitch was simple—the Methodist Mining Company would pay dividends in heaven as well as on earth. Unfortunately, the financing scheme collapsed before work on the church was completed. Lander County briefly acquired the church to settle outstanding debts before selling it back to the congregation. Reportedly, the good reverend left town while this was all happening. Today, the church, located a block north of Main Street at 135 Court Street, serves as Austin's community center and is open for special events and town meetings.

Another Austin landmark, St. George's Episcopal Church at 156 Main Street, was built in 1878 and is the only one of the town's historic houses of worship that is still used for church services each Sunday morning. The building is said to have been paid for from money collected on a single day, Easter Sunday 1877. The largest donation was a pledge of $9,500, which was contributed by a local mine superintendent. Two parishioners donated a 900-pound bell for the church. The bell was made in New York and contains silver that was mined in Austin (which is said to give the bell a "silvery" tone). St. George's still has its original pipe organ, which traveled around Cape

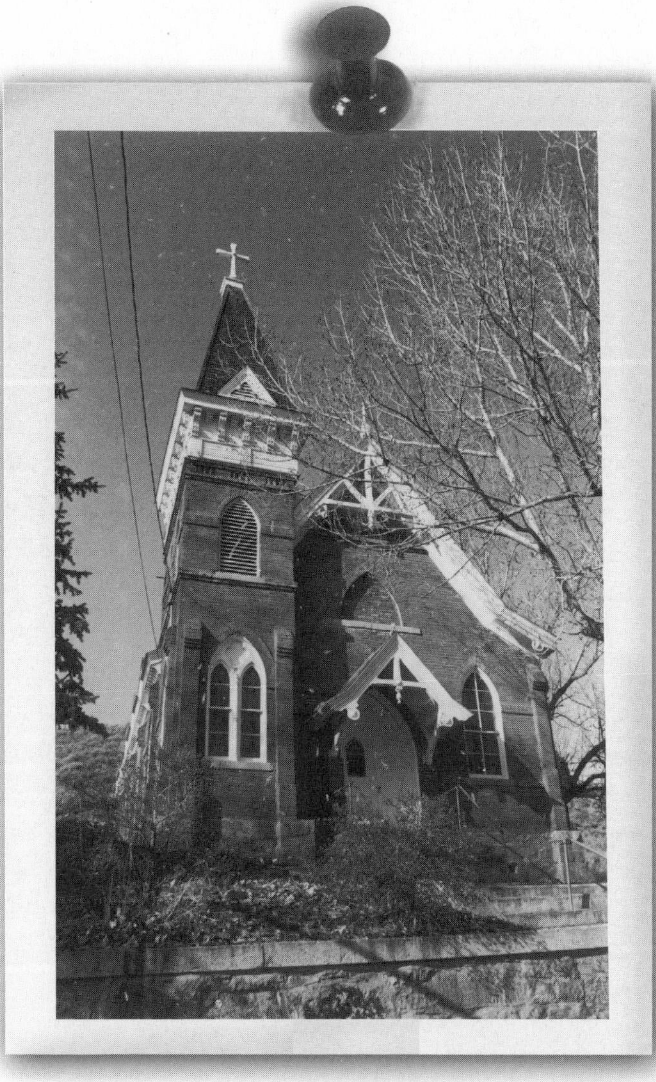

Atheists were out of place in Austin, a town of big churches.

Horn by ship to San Francisco and was brought to Austin by wagon. A rather unique feature of the church is that the entrance to the bell tower is also a bathroom. A person must stand on top of the toilet to reach the rope that rings the bell.

The town's third main house of worship, St. Augustine's Catholic Church, is the oldest church in town. Erected in 1866, it was used for services for nearly a century. One of the more cautionary tales told about the church is that a couple of years ago, its bell tower was threatened with collapse because nesting pigeons had relieved themselves there for decades. The weight of tons of guano in the tower was causing the ceiling to buckle. Just when all seemed lost, a local handyman, who had a recurring problem with alcohol, appeared in front of the local magistrate. His sentence was to shovel out the massive accumulation of bird droppings. No one knows if the man ever had a drink again. A nonprofit group recently acquired the church, located north of Main Street at 113 Virginia Street, and is raising funds to restore the building as a cultural center.

The World's Most Profitable Sack of Flour

Austin

April 19, 1864, was Election Day in Austin. For the occasion, two prominent local businessmen, store owner Reuel Gridley and Doctor Herrick, agreed to a wager that should the local mayoral candidate supported by either man win, the other would carry a 50-pound sack of flour through the main street of the town while whistling a political tune. Unfortunately for Gridley, Herrick's candidate won, so a few weeks after the election, amidst great fanfare, the shopkeeper hoisted a sack of flour on his shoulder and began his walk through town, while whistling "Old John Brown." A parade of local officials, the local band, and others on horseback formed a procession and led Gridley through the community. Nearly everyone in Austin came out to watch the spectacle, which had taken on the aura of a celebration.

Following the 1-mile trek, many gave speeches, and Gridley auctioned the sack of flour, with the proceeds going to the Sanitary Fund, the Civil War–era predecessor to the Red Cross. After the sack was sold, its buyer returned it to Gridley, who was encouraged to auction it again. This ritual continued for the rest of the day. By the conclusion of the auction, more than $4,000 had been raised for charity.

Other communities heard about Gridley's famous sack of flour, and he was invited to conduct similar auctions throughout Nevada and the West. During the next year Gridley traveled to places like Virginia City and raised an estimated $275,000 for the aid fund. Gridley, however, was a better promoter than he was a businessman. Because of his frequent absences from the store, the business took a downturn, and he was forced to close it (the structure is still standing in Austin and has been converted into a local museum). As for the boomeranging sack of flour, in the early twentieth century it was donated by his family to the Nevada Historical Society in Reno, which has it on display. The Historical Society is located at 1650 North Virginia Street, just north of the University of Nevada–Reno campus. It's open Monday through Saturday, 10:00 a.m. to 5:00 p.m. Admission is $3 for adults, $2 for seniors; kids are admitted free. For information call (775) 688-1190 or go to www.nevadaculture.org/docs/museums/Reno/his-soc.htm.

The Loneliest Art Collection on the Loneliest Road

Eureka

About three decades ago, Wally Cuchine bought his first piece of art by a Nevada artist. At the time, he was working as a humanities scholar in the central Nevada town of Hawthorne and discovered a small artist colony in the community. Because most of them were relatively unknown, he purchased a number of pieces at relatively little cost, although he likes to point out that back then even a $25 piece of art was a lot of money for him.

Since then, you could say he has evolved into a bit of a collector. Today, Cuchine owns more than 400 individual pieces and has compiled what has been described as the largest private collection of Nevada artwork. The works include paintings by Larry Jacox, Jeff Nicholson, Ron Arthaud, and Jack Malotte as well as sculptures and mixed-media works. And given that Cuchine is not wealthy, he has even purchased some of the pieces on monthly payment plans.

The collection has grown so large that it fills nearly every square inch of Cuchine's two mobile homes in the former mining town of Eureka, where he serves as director of the Eureka Opera House. He has converted one of the trailers into what he calls the Shed Gallery. In fact, if you stop by the Opera House (31 South Main Street; 775-237-6040) to meet Cuchine, more often than not he is eager to take visitors to his gallery to check out his collection.

In 2005 the Nevada Historical Society was so impressed by Cuchine's collection that it exhibited more than sixty pieces in a show entitled "Wally's World: The Loneliest Art Collection in Nevada." Cuchine, who is in his late fifties, says that someday he will donate his collection to a public institution, where people will be able to admire the works that are his passion.

Eureka's Underground

Eureka

For years there have been stories and legends about a series of tunnels beneath the historic mining town of Eureka. Some claimed that they were secret opium dens operated by the community's once-sizable Chinese population. Others said that they were built for flood protection or so that merchants could get to work from their homes without walking through the town's muddy streets. Nevada historical writer David W. Toll has said that the tunnels were built because the local breweries were located on opposite ends of town, and during the winter, when the streets were muddy or covered with wet snow, it was easier to roll kegs from the breweries to the saloons via a dry tunnel. He said they were also used by schoolchildren get to and from school and notes that former Nevada governor Reinhold Sadler, who owned a two-story house in town, had a tunnel built to get from his home to his store on Main Street. In Toll's *The Complete Nevada Traveler,* he notes, "In its heyday it [the tunneling] was quite comfortable to use, fancy, even, with brick walls, and arched brick chambers reminiscent of medieval dungeons."

Photo courtesy of the Nevada Historical Society

What went on in Eureka's mysterious underground tunnels?

The tunnels have been featured in a couple of fictional novels. Writer Carol Davis Luce's *Night Passages* is a mystery in which much of the action takes place in an elaborate tunnel system said to be below the town of Eureka. In Luce's novel, a murderer is able to roam the town without being seen or captured because he knows of the tunnels and is able to access them.

These days, however, most of the tunneling has collapsed, has been filled in, or is marginally safe. Wally Cuchine, director of the Eureka Opera House, has been inside a portion of the tunnel below a downtown business and describes it as having an elegant, arched brick ceiling with brick walls. He said the tunnels look more like interconnected basements between various downtown businesses than a series of long, narrow passages. And he said they look extremely old and unsafe.

So no guided tours in the immediate future.

Fort Fear

Fort Churchill

Fort Churchill was built during a time of fear. The adobe complex was constructed in 1860 by the federal government to provide a home for a garrison of troops thought necessary to protect western Nevada settlers, who were fearful of an Indian uprising. Earlier that year, local tribes had fought with the white settlers in the so-called

Photo: Elissa Curtis.

Better to have a fort and not need it—no shot was ever fired in anger at Fort Churchill.

Pyramid Lake War. The dispute started after three white men kidnapped two Indian women at a place called Williams Station, located about 30 miles east of Carson City. A group of Indians discovered the treachery and responded by rescuing the women and burning the station. Stories about the raid began to circulate—and naturally became exaggerated. A short time after the Williams Station attack, a group of 105 volunteer civilian soldiers gathered in Virginia City to march on the Indians. The ill-prepared Virginia City war party encountered the Indians in a small valley located a few miles south of Pyramid Lake. About two-thirds of the volunteers perished in the conflict. The victory led to retaliation by regular army troops. At a second battle near Pyramid Lake, the outnumbered Indians were defeated. To prevent further unrest, the U.S. government decided to build the fort, one of the most expensive ever constructed because of its remote location. The show of military might was also supposed to deter the Indians from attacking Pony Express riders, who were occasionally chased by Indians resentful of their passing through lands traditionally controlled by local tribes.

Once things died down between the settlers and the Indians, the fort became a western outpost for the U.S. Army during the Civil War. Although the Nevada garrison was never called into action, it was an important training ground and supply depot for the Nevada Military District. In 1869 the U.S. government decided to abandon the post, which was expensive to operate, and auction the buildings. The wooden roofs, supports, and porches were removed and sold, but the adobe walls remained. Wood from the fort was used to build Buckland's Station, a stagecoach stop and hotel, which still stands about a mile east of the fort.

Although some efforts were made in the 1930s to preserve the buildings, it wasn't until 1957 that the site was acquired by the State of Nevada for a state historic park. Since then, the state has stabilized the buildings in a condition of "arrested decay." Today, visitors can sometimes observe workers placing new adobe bricks that are manufactured from local clay onto the walls. On a bluff overlooking the fort site is an excellent visitor center—a whitewashed, wood-shingled building that resembles one of the original structures. Below the fort, in a cottonwood grove on the banks of the Carson River, is a developed camping and picnicking area. The fort is located 40 miles east of Carson City via US 50 and Alternate US 93. For more information call (775) 577-2345 or go to www.parks.nv.gov/fc.htm.

The Road of Death

40 Mile Desert

Imagine it's the late 1840s and that you've left your home in Missouri or Illinois to head to California's goldfields. After traveling more than halfway across the United States, including Nebraska, Wyoming, and Utah, you reach Nevada. Your party follows the meandering Humboldt River for several hundred miles across the state and reaches a place called Big Meadows (Lovelock), where, it seems, you're finally on the last leg of the long, long journey.

And then you reach the 40 Mile Desert.

This stretch of dry, alkali flatland northwest of Fallon was considered one of the most difficult stretches on the entire Emigrant Trail. It had no trees, no drinkable water, no grass—no Starbucks. It was 40 miles of flat terrain with patches of thick, sticky mud that bogged down travelers. Emigrant diaries, such as this 1849 entry by Jasper M. Hixson, tell the story best: "For some distance the surrounding flats were almost impassable, not swampy as one would understand by the word, but rotten. With great difficulty we passed over this place, wagons sinking to the bed, mules miring, etc."

During this part of the journey, travelers often lost their livestock and wagons, tossed aside their belongings, and sometimes were unable to continue. Emigrant diaries record that abandoned wagons littered the trail and that dead animals were numerous. Goods ranging from the substantial, such as pianos, to lighter items, like books, guns, clothing, pans, and dishes, were strewn throughout the desert.

In 1850 traveler George Willis Read wrote, "I saw 200 wagons in a half-mile and dead animals so thick you could step from one to another." Along the road there were also dozens of graves, usually simple mounds marked with crude headboards crafted from abandoned scraps of wood. Most travelers made the crossing in about twenty-four hours—the longest day of their lives. At the end of the ordeal, the stragglers arrived at the Carson River, where they could finally find water and grass for their animals.

For those wanting to retrace this dreadful stretch of real estate, take a drive on US 95, between Interstate 80 and Fallon, which borders the eastern part of the 40 Mile Desert. A historic marker at the intersection of I-80 and US 95 marks the beginning of the desert. And as you race along in your air-conditioned vehicle and view all that dry, alkali nothingness, think about what James Carpenter wrote in 1852: "We were so nearly famished for water that our tongues were Black and neither could talk. We got to the river and such water we could not drink our tongues were so swolen [*sic*] but we burried [*sic*] our faces in the clear bright water guzeled [*sic*] it up as best we could then waited a few minutes and guzel [*sic*] again."

Thank goodness there's a McDonald's in Fallon.

The Sole Tree

Middlegate

Travelers on US 50 encounter an unusual sight—a giant cottonwood near Middlegate filled with pairs of hanging shoes. There are several versions of the story behind the tree, but according to a 1998 Associated Press article, in the early 1990s a young couple from Oregon had gone to Reno to get married. Fredda Stevenson, co-owner of the nearby Middlegate Station bar, told the AP: "They camped by the tree. They had their first big fight. The girl threatened to walk to Oregon. He took her shoes, tied the laces in a knot and threw them up in the tree. He said, 'If you're going to walk home, you're going to have to climb a tree first.'"

A tree with a lot of sole—the Old Shoe Tree

She said that the husband "drove down here and we talked for two or three hours. I told him to go back and say he was sorry and that it was all his fault." She said the man took her advice, and the couple made up and drove away. A year later they stopped by to show off their first child, whose first pair of shoes now hangs in the tree.

Trivia

The Name Says It All

Though never really much of a town, Ragtown was the name of the settlement and trading post that developed on the banks of the Carson River, a few miles west of Fallon. In Thompson and West's *History of Nevada* (1881), two reasons are given for the origins of the name: "One is that it was originally composed of cloth houses built by traders from California, who leaving in the fall, left their ragged shelters to flutter in the wind. According to another authority, the emigrants, on reaching it, hastened to divest themselves of their ragged garments, and plunge into the cooling waters of the Carson. Long, scattered piles of rags daily adorned the banks of that stream."

Historical records indicate that Ragtown was one of the first trading posts founded on the Emigrant Trail. Its location at the end of the 40 Mile Desert made it an ideal place for those who survived the difficult trek to restock and resupply. After 1854, Asa Kenyon operated the Kenyon Farm Station, which offered fresh produce, beef, and other goods. Unfortunately, many did not live through the journey across the desert, so Ragtown was also the site of one of the state's earliest graveyards. Reportedly, more than 200 pioneers were buried near the town; most were victims of "cholera, fever and exhaustion in early years, and their graves were variously marked with log-chains, wagon-tires, etc.," according to Thompson and West. Today, a historic marker on US 50 notes the spot of the former trading post.

Over time, others saw the shoes in the cottonwood, which is about 70 feet tall, and began tossing their own footwear into its branches. These days, there are dozens of leather and canvas sneakers, oxfords, pumps, cowboy boots, wingtips, slippers, sandals, and other footgear hanging from the Old Shoe Tree. In addition, others have tossed a plastic pink flamingo and a couple of bras into the tree.

A few years ago, someone even nailed a small, sock-shaped plaque to the tree, which said in part:

> The largest Shoe Tree in the world . . .
> My friend as you're driving by
> Would you leave a pair of shoes
> Fore now you have aplenty
> So what have you to lose.

The Old Shoe Tree is located adjacent to US 50, about 48 miles east of Fallon (about a mile east of the tiny outpost of Middlegate) or 110 miles east of Reno via U.S. Highway 395 and US 50.

Mother Nature's Cistern

Monitor Valley

Few of Nevada's geologic sites are as unexpected as Diana's Punchbowl, a 600-foot-high, white travertine hill with a wide, deep hole in the top that is filled with scalding hot water. Surrounded by miles of open space in the middle of the Monitor Valley, the chalky hill is easy to spot. And when you stand on top of it, looking into the wide mouth of the beast, it can be a bit unsettling. The hole measures about 50 feet across, and inside are steep, nearly vertical walls that drop down about 30 feet to a small geothermal pool filled with water that is said to be 200 degrees (Fahrenheit) and reportedly exhales hot vapors and gases as well as steam.

Yet despite its remote location in a seemingly untouched landscape, Diana's Punchbowl hasn't been immune to the less desirable aspects of modern civilization—graffiti has been painted on one of its interior walls, and a couple of old beer bottles and soda cans lie on a grassy ledge above the pool. (What kind of idiot desecrates a place such as this?)

Standing at the lip of the bowl, looking down into the blue-green waters, you can't help but be impressed by the size and appearance of this marvel. Geologically, the bowl seems to have been created when the top and center core of this limestone hill collapsed, leaving behind the large, water-filled opening. The origins of the bowl's name vary. Helen Carlson's book *Nevada Place Names* implies that the name came from Diana, the Roman goddess of springs and brooks.

According to Phillip I. Earl, former curator of history at the Nevada Historical Society, native people in the region have known of the site for thousands of years, and local ranchers have been aware of it since their arrival in the 1860s. Earl has written that the Native Americans viewed the bowl as the home of great spirits, lost souls, and mysterious creatures. He noted that one particularly common story surrounds the tossing of an unfaithful husband into the steaming-hot bowl by his unhappy wife—although there's another version of the story that has a jealous husband dropping his wife (named Diana) into the hot water after suspecting her of infidelity.

The first tourists to visit the site were probably local folks from nearby Belmont, Austin, or Tonopah, who, according to Earl, would picnic on the mound's slopes and enjoy the views. Earl has also written that a bottle thrown into the bowl's hot waters will break as it touches the surface—but don't try it because littering is against the law. Diana's Punchbowl is located about 35 miles south of US 50 via a dirt road that is 13 miles east of the Hickison Summit Rest Stop. Just look for the big white hill.

The World's Biggest Sandbox

Sand Mountain Recreation Area

Perhaps the best way to describe Sand Mountain is that it's a big beach without an ocean. Located 32 miles east of Fallon on US 50, Sand Mountain is in reality a massive sand dune that rises about 600

Is Sand Mountain the world's biggest outdoor volleyball court?

feet above the desert floor. The dune was formed from sand from the surrounding flats, which were once part of an ancient inland sea called Lake Lahontan. About 4,000 years ago, the lake dried up, leaving behind the sandy lake bottom. Over centuries, the dried sand was blown against nearby Stillwater Range, accumulating into a huge mound. Not surprisingly, the mountain and surrounding area have become a recreational playland. The mountain is an off-road enthusiast's delight. On any given day, the dune is dotted with specialized two-, three-, and four-wheel motorized bikes and dune buggies skirting across its sandy surface.

It has also become a haven for extreme athletes participating in the relatively new sport known as sandboarding. Basically, sandboarding is riding down the dune's slopes on a smooth-bottomed sandboard at very high speeds—kind of like snowboarding on sand. The mountain, in fact, has become so renowned for its speedy slopes that each fall some of the world's most experienced sandboarders compete in the Sand Mountain Open. In recent years boarders have achieved speeds in excess of 45 miles per hour during some of their runs. In addition to hosting all those sand-recreationalists, the mountain has certain other, unique qualities. For instance, it produces a booming sound when you walk on it (the sound is said to be a result of air being pushed through the sand by your weight), and at night when the wind blows across the sand, the mountain is said to be singing. According to Native American legend, the booming noise was made by the god of the dune as a warning to stay away.

Unintended Consequences

Soda Lake

Soda Lake looks like dozens of other small desert bodies of water. It doesn't have much vegetation around the edges, and its waters seem kind of murky and uninviting. But, as with many things, there's literally much more beneath the surface—in this case, a ghostly forest of cottonwood trees and the remains of an old soda factory.

Soda Lake's story began in 1855, when pioneer Asa Kenyon discovered a depression on the edge of the 40 Mile Desert that appeared to be covered by a large sheet of ice. Upon closer inspection, he found that the white surface was a deposit of nearly pure soda, a substance useful in mining and for producing soap, glass, and paper. According to Thompson and West's *History of Nevada* (1881), Kenyon had stumbled upon Soda Lake, "an oval area of about 16 acres, having a depression of 75-feet below the general level. It cannot be seen until the visitor almost reaches its rim." Several natural springs flowed into the depression, including one from the north side that contained about 33 percent soda.

From the 1860s until the early twentieth century, Soda Lake produced tons of soda. Two soda-manufacturing plants were erected in the 1870s on the edge of the lake. Records indicate that soda from the lake was of such quality that it was awarded a gold medal at the 1876 Centennial Exposition in Philadelphia. Unfortunately for the soda plants, the completion of the Newlands Water Project in 1915—which spurred the development of the surrounding Lahontan

Beneath Soda Lake are unexpected sights—like a grove of trees.

Valley and the city of Fallon—caused their demise. Irrigation water from the extensive aqueduct system, which turned the area into an agricultural and ranching oasis, also made the groundwater level rise. Within a few years the soda works were submerged, an occurrence that resulted in several lawsuits, including a landmark legal decision stating that the U.S. government could be absolved from damages as a result of "unintentional" actions committed by one of its agencies. In the end, the lake level rose from 147 feet to more than 200 feet, leaving the soda works under some 35 feet of water. Since then, the lake has become popular with divers, who can swim through the relatively intact ruins of the old soda plant and other buildings. Divers also report the presence of a "ghost forest" at the southeastern end of the lake; this forest is the remains of cottonwoods that once grew on the banks of the original lake.

Because of its undeveloped nature—submerged soda plants notwithstanding—the lake, located about 55 miles east of Carson City via US 50 and Soda Lake Road, has become a sanctuary for a wide variety of birds. Visitors can often spot flocks of gulls, terns, ducks, and other waterfowl enjoying the peace and calm of this half-hidden lake. The lake also boasts a population of brine shrimp and underwater plants that have adapted to the high alkali content of the water. Geologically speaking, the Soda Lake basin was created by a collapsed volcanic cone. The outline of the cone can best be seen on the east side of the lake, where it rises high above the water. On the ground around the lake, rock hounds can find plenty of stones that are volcanic in origin.

The Painted Cave

Toquima Cave

Located in central Nevada, Toquima Cave is an archaeologically significant site that contains prehistoric pictographs, which are symbols, designs, and patterns painted on the cave walls. Pictographs are similar to petroglyphs, which have been carved into rock rather than painted. Archaeologists aren't quite sure how to interpret them, but it is generally believed that Native American people, who may have been the ancestors to today's Nevada tribes, created the drawings and carvings and that this artwork may have had some type of religious significance.

The pictographs inside Toquima Cave appear in many shapes and patterns and use a variety of colors. Rock walls are marked with strange round shapes as well as different kinds of squiggly and straight lines. Despite their age—these pictures are believed to be at least 1,000 years old—the red, yellow, white, and black colors remain impressive and bright. If you look closely at the symbols, they begin to take on familiar forms. A couple of lines and circles become a stick figure of a deer or elk. Another cluster of lines looks like an elephant—although elephants never lived in Nevada—or maybe a bison. The sheer number of pictographs is surprising—there appear to be dozens drawn all over the cave walls.

Of course, it is natural to speculate about what they mean. Maybe they tell stories or convey some kind of information from one generation to the next. Perhaps they are just cave graffiti or represent some kind of record-keeping system—a prehistoric shopping list? But what are they doing in such an out-of-the-way place? Why would someone climb all the way to this cave just to scribble on the walls? The answer may be in the landscape. Looking out from the cave, you see a spectacular view of the surrounding valley and the thickets of piñon trees. Maybe those ancient people came to the cave simply because it was a cool place to hang out and enjoy the view. It seems as good a reason as any.

A 10-foot-high cyclone fence protects the cave, so the only way to see its interior is when the National Forest Service conducts a guided tour. For a tour schedule visit the Forest Service's Tonopah Ranger District Web site (www.fs.fed.us/r4/htnf/districts/tonopah.shtm). The nearby Toquima Cave Campground is open from May to November. It has only six sites; two have picnic tables. One of the sites has a fire pit with a grill, while the others have fire rings. There is a unisex toilet near the campground but no water or garbage facilities, so bring any food and water needed (and pack all garbage out).

To reach Toquima Cave, travel about 14 miles east of Austin on US 50 to the junction with Route 376 (the road to Tonopah). Turn south on Route 376; after about 0.1 mile, take an immediate left onto a dirt road (marked by a historical marker for Toquima Cave). Continue for about 15 miles across the valley and head into the mountains.

At a place known as Pete's Summit, you'll reach the Toquima Caves Campground (it is marked with large Forest Service signs). Park near the campgrounds, and then hike about 0.25 mile on a marked trail to the cave. It's best to plan your visit during the summer or fall because the roads can be impassable in the wetter months. The hike to the cave winds through a forest of scruffy piñon trees. The trail gradually climbs to a large red-colored rock outcropping, where the cave is located. You'll know you've found it when you spot the tall metal fence across the mouth of the cave.

The Fibbing Festival

Yerington

In the nineteenth century it was sometimes difficult to tell the truth from fiction in many Nevada newspapers. Fabricated stories—including many by humorist Mark Twain—were a tradition among these publications. In fact, in 1873 the editor of Austin's newspaper, *The Reese River Reveille,* concocted stories about a nonexistent social club dedicated to telling tall tales, the Sazerac Lying Club. In the first article the editor, Fred Hart, described the election of club officers—all real people living in Austin—and shared a few of the colorful lies allegedly told during the first meeting. The response was so positive that for months afterward the paper entertained its readers with tales of the wild lies and outrageous claims made by club members during their regular meetings. Soon, other western newspapers picked up the articles, and eventually Austin's famed fibbing club was the

The Loneliest Road in America

In 1986 *Life* magazine described US 50 across the center of Nevada as the "Loneliest Road in America." The magazine said that in particular the 287-mile stretch of road between Fernley and Ely was remote, with few points of interest, and it urged travelers to have "survival skills" to make the journey. In response, the communities along the route—Ely, Eureka, Austin, Fallon, and Fernley—worked with the Nevada Commission on Tourism to develop a tongue-in-cheek "Highway 50 Survival Kit" containing brochures and maps detailing places on the highway. Additionally, a road game was created that urged travelers to stop in each of the communities to have a Highway 50 map stamped by a local business or chamber of commerce. The validated maps could be redeemed for an official "Loneliest Road Survivor" certificate and other souvenirs. In 1988 the Nevada legislature even officially declared US 50 across Nevada as the "Loneliest Road in America" and had official signs posted across the state.

So, is it really the loneliest road in America? Not according to the Nevada Department of Transportation, which reports an average of about 650 vehicles per day at its loneliest point, near Austin. In fact, US 50 is not even the loneliest road in Nevada. For example, Route 121 from US 50 to the Dixie Valley gets a mere 10 cars per day in both directions. Route 722 from Eastgate to Austin—the original route of US 50 in the center of the state—sees a total of 45 vehicles a day.

US 50 is also one of the state's most historic routes. In 1859 Captain James H. Simpson led a U.S. Army Topographical Corps mapping expedition along the route. His findings helped the founders of the Pony Express select that route when they established their legendary mail service a year later. Although the Pony Express stayed in business only for about eighteen months, the road (as well as many of

Bring your own company if you're crossing the "Loneliest Road in America."

the Pony Express stations) was soon incorporated into the Overland Stagecoach and Mail line. In the early twentieth century, the central Nevada route was chosen to be part of the first transcontinental automobile road, the Lincoln Highway. In the 1920s the Lincoln Highway was absorbed into the federal highway system and became US 50.

It's easy to become a proud survivor of a journey on the "Loneliest Road." The Nevada Tourism department continues to mail out hundreds of Survival Kits each month—in fact, the package was spruced up a few years ago for the twentieth anniversary of the *Life* story. To get a free kit just call (800) NEVADA-8 or go to www.travelnevada.com.

subject of a book collecting Hart's articles. The joke came to an end in 1877, when Hart decided to leave the paper and move to Virginia City. He wrote a final story about the club's dissolution—ending the existence of a club that never actually existed.

Even though Hart's Sazerac Lying Club didn't actually exist, in 2006 another Nevada community decided to resurrect his idea. On April Fool's Day of that year, the town of Yerington hosted the First Occasional Lyon County Liar's Contest. The event attracted more than one hundred people, who listened to tall tales about ghosts, animals, fish, and other subjects. The event raised money for the nonprofit Silver Springs Spay and Neuter Project.

The event's organizer, Tom Blomquist, said he was inspired to create the contest after reading about the legendary Sazerac Lying Club and noticing that the original seal for Lyon County featured a bull and a shovel. Judges for the event ranged from a local judge to the madam of the Moonlite Bunny Ranch, a Lyon County brothel. And the winner was a man who was running for sheriff at the time. Charlie Duke, portraying a character he called Jeremiah B. Lyon, claimed that he was more than 180 years old and told stories about the early days of Yerington, when it was little more than a saloon called Pizen Switch. For his effort Duke won $400 and a Moonlite Bunny Ranch bathrobe. Presumably he didn't wear the robe while campaigning, but he did lose the election.

CHAPTER

6

North
Interstate 80

"You know you have arrived at Battle Mountain because the town has marked its identity on a nearby hill in enormous letters fashioned from whitewashed rock. I have returned to this place to find in it not America's armpit, but America's heart. I am here to mine the good in it, to tell the world that Battle Mountain doesn't stink. That is my new challenge. I hang a right off the highway at the base of the hill, which proudly proclaims, in giant letters: BM Man. This is not going to be easy."

—Gene Weingarten, *Washington Post* (2001)

Years ago, Pulitzer *Prize–winning feature writer Gene Weingarten asked his* Washington Post *readers to nominate a community that should be considered the "Armpit of America." Battle Mountain, Nevada, won the dubious distinction. Not that Battle Mountain is that bad. After visiting, even Weingarten admitted to being charmed by the place, mostly because of the friendliness of the locals. And that, in fact, is what defines Nevada's small towns, particularly those along Interstate 80. Communities such as Lovelock, Winnemucca, Wells, and—yes—Battle Mountain are places where people put up pictures of their lost dog—and it gets returned safely—and where people who tell you to have a nice day aren't trying to convert you to a new religion. Even though the towns may lack a few amenities—or a lot of amenities—they often have other, more interesting attributes.*

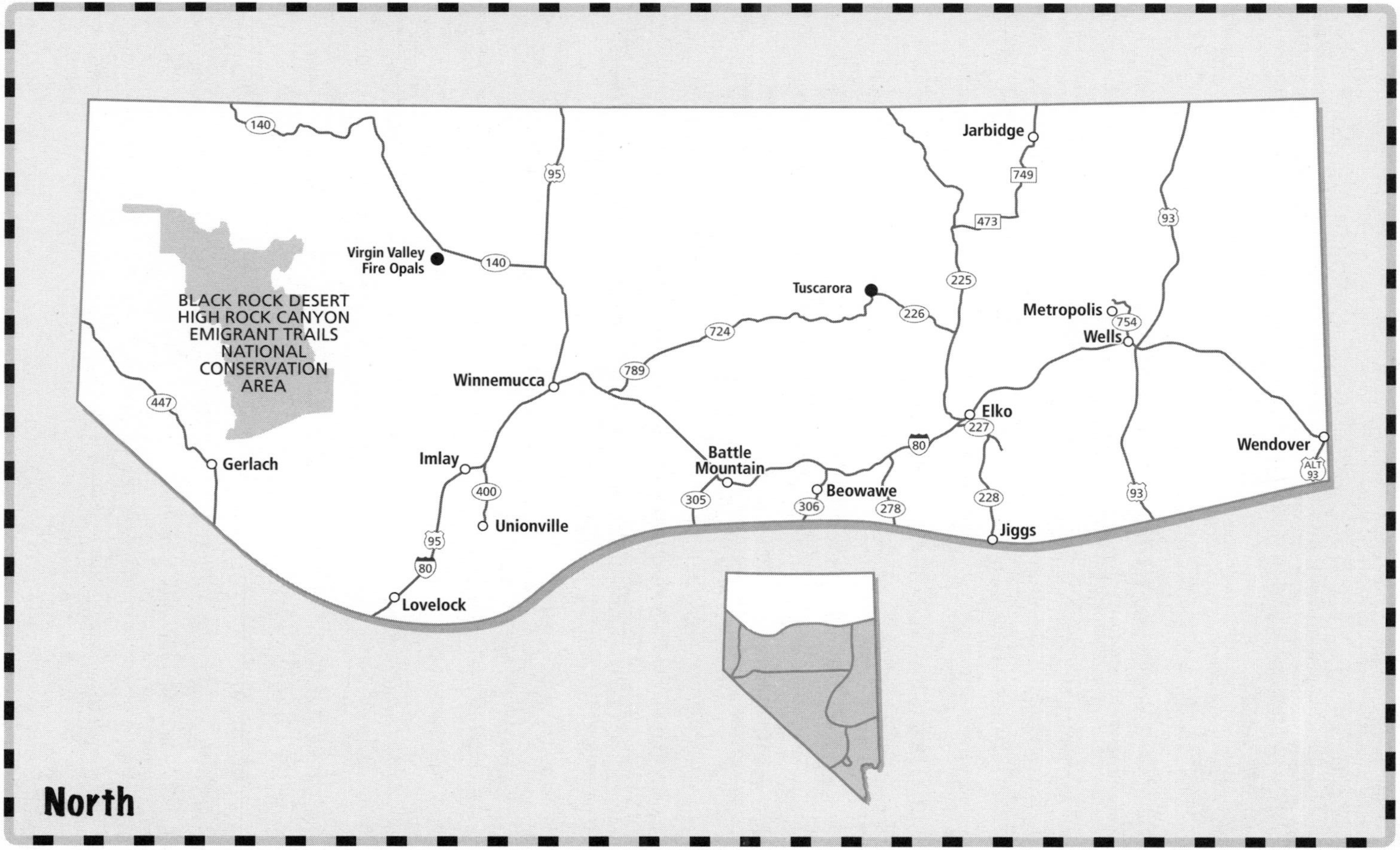

North
BLACK ROCK DESERT HIGH ROCK CANYON EMIGRANT TRAILS NATIONAL CONSERVATION AREA
Virgin Valley Fire Opals
Tuscarora
Jarbidge
Metropolis
Wells
Winnemucca
Elko
Wendover
Gerlach
Imlay
Battle Mountain
Beowawe
Unionville
Jiggs
Lovelock
140
95
447
400
80
789
724
226
225
473
749
93
754
227
228
278
306
305
ALT 93

Flat and Boring Can Be Good

Battle Mountain

It's not often that something ordinary and mundane can thrust a place into prominence. But that's exactly what happened near the north-central Nevada town of Battle Mountain, which, it was discovered, is the site of a 4-mile stretch of frontage road so straight and flat that it is the ideal place to race human-powered vehicles.

About a decade ago, the Human Powered Vehicle Association determined that Route 305, just outside Battle Mountain, is "one of the straightest, flattest and smoothest surfaces in the world." In 1999 the group, which oversees the setting of speed records made by human-powered vehicles, began hosting the World Human-Powered Speed Challenge in Battle Mountain.

Since then, dozens of riders, most racing customized recumbents (bicycle-like devices ridden in the seated or supine position) made of high-tech, lightweight materials, have flocked to Battle Mountain to attempt to break world records for pedal-powered vehicles. In the rarefied high desert air (the altitude is 4,619 feet), dozens of new records have been set and shattered over the years. Riders have an acceleration zone of about 4 miles in which to reach their maximum velocity before being timed crossing the official 200-meter distance. Current world records set on the Battle Mountain course include American Sam Whittingham's sprint of 81 miles per hour in 2002, which set the world record for a solo rider; American Lisa Vetterlein's 2005 women's world speed record of 66.59 miles per hour; and Damjan Zabovnik's ride of 74.1 miles per hour in 2006, facing backwards, which allowed him to become the European human-powered vehicle champion.

Faster Than a Speeding Bullet

Man's need to achieve ever-faster speeds has never been more obvious than on Nevada's Black Rock Desert, located just north of the tiny hamlet of Gerlach. The desert is more than a million acres of emptiness. It is a desolate place of seemingly endless bone-white alkali flats bordered by rounded, barren-looking mountains. And it is flat. In fact, it's considered one of the flattest places in the world, which, of course, makes it one of the most ideal spots to try to drive really fast, particularly in the fall, when the alkali surface has had months to bake to nearly concrete hardness.

Over the years several attempts have been made in the Black Rock Desert to establish a new land speed record. On October 13, 1997, however, a British team succeeded in doing something no one had ever done before—racing a land-based vehicle so fast that it broke the sound barrier. The rocket-powered Thrust SSC car, driven by Andrew Green of England, shattered the barrier on October 13 and, two days later, surpassed that effort by making two runs averaging 763.035 miles per hour, faster than any land vehicle had ever gone. The second set of runs established a new official world land-speed record, which has not been broken.

Photo courtesy of the Nevada Commision on Tourism

One of the earth's flattest places, the Black Rock Desert is where the world land speed record was set in 1997.

Burning Man

Black Rock Desert

Based on some of the media attention that the annual Burning Man celebration receives, you might think the event is some kind of pagan-hippie-anarchist-druggie-nudist-apocalyptic-love-in-freakfest. Typical images show half-naked, brightly painted, and flamboyantly costumed men and women frolicking on the dusty flats of the Black Rock Desert in September. The coverage usually includes scenes of the traditional igniting of the Burning Man, the giant wooden figure of a man that is the symbol of the festival.

But those who attend and organize Burning Man insist that that's not an accurate picture. Although plenty of people are naked and half-naked or painted and swathed in outrageous attire, and there is the burning of a giant wooden man, the event is really "an endless spectacle of self-expression," according to founder Larry Harvey, writing on the event's Web site. "Burning Man is certainly a kind of party, but it is also a carefully crafted social experiment.

"We have tried to create an environment that functions as an incubator of the social process that gives rise to human culture and this, by extension, functions as a critique of society at large."

Of course, what Burning Man is depends on the participant. Artist/photographer Doug Keister once described the Black Rock Desert as a tabula rasa, or blank slate, and that's certainly true during Burning Man, which attracts nearly 50,000 people. Stockbrokers from San Francisco, organic farmers from Corvallis, and video game programmers from Provo can shed the trappings of their "normal" lives and, for a week, become part of Harvey's bold social experiment. The result is a kind of organized chaos in the desert. Which doesn't mean there aren't rules. One of the primary ones is to bring only what you need to survive in the desert and take everything you bring back out. The event eschews commercialism; nothing can be sold on the site.

The event started spontaneously in 1986, when Harvey and friend Jerry James built an 8-foot-tall wooden man figure on San Francisco's

Baker Beach in honor of the summer solstice and then burned it in front of about twenty friends. Some media stories claim that Harvey built and burned the figure because of a broken heart. Although the first burning did coincide with the anniversary of a failed relationship, he says the story is not true. During the next three years, Harvey and a growing number of friends, acquaintances, and interested bystanders returned to the beach to torch increasingly larger Burning Man figures. In 1990, however, the burning was relocated to the Black Rock Desert as a result of increasing tensions between the burners and San Francisco police.

Since then, the event has grown exponentially, attracting 250 participants during its first year in the desert, then jumping to 600 the next year, 1,000 the following year, and 8,000 by its tenth year. Over the years the celebration has expanded from the simple burning of the wooden figure into a full-scale arts festival that includes a fashion show, an on-site newspaper (*The Black Rock Gazette*), and Black Rock City, a massive temporary settlement complete with themed camps and villages. Throughout the year burners keep in touch via an interactive Web site, www.burningman.com.

Nevada's First Entertainment Capital Was . . . Elko?

Elko

The first place in Nevada to offer big-name entertainment wasn't in Las Vegas or Reno. It was the Commercial Hotel in the northeastern Nevada town of Elko. On April 26, 1941, Commercial Hotel owner Newt Crumley took a huge risk and hired bandleader Ted Lewis (whose famous catchphrase was "Is everybody happy?") and his orchestra for a one-week stand. At the time, the colorful Lewis, who always wore a battered top hat, was a major recording star who performed in nightclubs throughout the country. Crumley paid Lewis and his band $12,000 to appear in the hotel's lounge for a week—a significant amount of money considering that there was no such thing as a cover charge, no food was served, and a glass of beer was

Elko's Commercial Hotel is the unlikely birthplace of Nevada's modern entertainment industry.

a nickel. The bold move paid off with standing-room-only crowds and a casino filled with gamblers. Fortunately for Crumley, Lewis was also an avid gambler and during the week lost his paycheck and more. It's said that he signed an IOU promising to return for another engagement (he did later that year).

Crumley followed up by booking other big-name stars, including singer Sophie Tucker, comedian Chico Marx, and the bands of Jimmy Dorsey, Paul Whiteman, and Lawrence Welk. It wasn't long before the big hotels in Reno and Las Vegas noticed Crumley's formula for success and began booking their own entertainment. For the next decade the Commercial continued bringing in the world's most famous performers to the remote cow town of Elko. In the early 1950s Crumley, who grew up in Tonopah and Reno, sold the hotel and purchased the Holiday Hotel in Reno. He died in 1962 after a plane he was piloting crashed northeast of Tonopah in a freezing rainstorm.

These days, the Commercial Hotel (345 Fourth Street; 800-648-2345) is still open in Elko. A little worn around the edges, the hotel trades on its history and proudly promotes its role in starting the state's entertainment business. The hotel is also home to White King, a giant mounted polar bear (he stands 10 feet 4 inches) who has been on display near the main entrance since 1958. He serves as the hotel's mascot and is a reminder of the days when casinos used carnival-style gimmicks to attract customers. In fact, check out the Brand Room Buffet, where, in the 1950s, local ranchers burned their brands into the walls, including singer Bing Crosby, who once owned a large ranch north of Elko.

Buckaroo Bards

Elko

In the early 1980s a number of folklorists, including Hal Cannon, became interested in the early-twentieth-century tradition of cowboy poetry. Aware that decades earlier buckaroos would sometimes recite poems about their lives, loves, hopes, and dreams, these folklorists decided to find out if the practice had died out. In January 1985 Cannon invited a few dozen working cowboys, all of whom had indicated that they recited cowboy poetry, to a gathering in Elko. In a later essay Cannon said that after he and Elko cowboy poet Waddie Mitchell put out 200 chairs for visitors, Mitchell said, "Hey, pard, we should put some of these chairs away. This is going to be embarrassing."

As it turned out, Mitchell was wrong. The event attracted more than 1,500 people and convinced Cannon that cowboy poetry was alive and well, albeit under the cultural radar. In the decades since, the cowboy poetry movement has grown; hundreds of similar gather-

Photo courtesy of the Nevada Commission on Tourism

Cowboy poetry ain't no whim, especially when sung by Sourdough Slim.

ings are held each year, and dozens of books and recordings have appeared. These days, the annual Elko recital—now known as the National Cowboy Poetry Gathering—is a weeklong event that draws thousands of visitors at the end of January. For tickets or information about the event, go to www.westernfolklife.org.

The art of cowboy poetry is generally believed to have started because being a cowboy on the range is a solitary life. So when buckaroos came together for a meal around a campfire, they began telling stories about their days, sometimes in rhyme or song. Many of the poems involved daily work, such as chasing a stray cow, scaring off coyotes, or breaking a horse. Sometimes they were humorous, playful, or even crude. And always they were authentic expressions of the cowhand's thoughts and feelings.

Or, as cowboy poet Jane Morton (not all cowboy poets are men) wrote:

We must tell the stories,
So memories live on,
Past time when the tellers
Themselves are long gone.

Nevada's Not-So-Natural Geyser

Fly Geyser

At first glance, Fly Geyser, located on the edge of the Black Rock Desert, about two hours north of Reno, is a spectacular sight as it spews clouds of hot water about 4 or 5 feet high in the air. The geyser consists of three, large travertine mounds that rise out of a field of tall reeds and grasses, with a series of terraces around the base. In addition to the spraying hot water, the most impressive thing about the trio of tufa rock cones is their colors—rich, vivid shades of green and rust.

And the whole thing is the result of an accident. The geyser was actually created in 1964, after a geothermal power company drilled a test well at the site. According to newspaper reports, the well either was left uncapped or was improperly plugged. As a result, the scalding hot water was allowed to blast uncontrolled from the well hole, and calcium carbonate deposits began to form, growing several inches each year. Now, after a few decades, those deposits have become large mounds taller than an average-size man. Scientists say that the green and reddish coloring on the outside of the mounds is the result of thermophilic algae, which flourish in moist, hot environments.

Interestingly, the set of circumstances that created Fly Geyser in 1964 apparently occurred at least one time before. In about 1917 a well was drilled a few hundred feet north of the geyser. This well was also abandoned, and over time a massive 10- to 12-foot-high calcium carbonate cone formed. Today, no hot water flows from the older mound—apparently the earlier geyser dried up when water was naturally diverted to the newer one. The geyser, which is about 20 miles north of Gerlach via Route 34, is located on private property (don't trespass), but the water plumes are easily visible from the road. Adjacent is a small geothermal pond, fed by runoff from the geyser.

Photo courtesy of the Nevada Commission on Tourism

One of Nevada's oddest "natural" wonders is the man-made Fly Geyser on the edge of the Black Rock Desert.

Set in Stone

Gerlach

DeWayne "Doobie" Williams was one-of-a-kind. Williams, who died in 1995, spent the last two decades or so of his life carving clever, pithy, and even bizarre comments onto large boulders lining a dirt road on the edge of the Black Rock Desert about 4 miles north of Gerlach, just off Route 34 (there is a sign on the left marked GURU ROAD). Williams also crafted weird art pieces from animal bones, scraps of wood, and assorted trash to visually enhance some of his sayings. He named the site of his creations Guru Road or Dooby Avenue.

Williams, who was born near Gerlach and earned his nickname, Doobie, because apparently he did inhale, modestly began his effort one day when he started chiseling his name onto a rock. Because the work was hard on the hands, he later shortened his nickname to "Dooby" to save a letter. Pleased with the results, he added stones with the names of friends and local residents. His inspiration for carving words in stone apparently came after hiking through High Rock Canyon, located north of Gerlach, where many early emigrants had carved their initials and the date of their passing.

Soon, Williams was placing the carved stones along a Bureau of Land Management road on the eastern side of the Granite Mountains, located a few miles north of Gerlach. He also began to expand his messages, writing brief, thought-provoking passages on the rocks. For example, on one rock he carved, "The human race is like a watch, it takes all the parts to make it work," while on another he wrote, "To crush the simple atom all mankind was intent, and now the atom will return the compliment." Others opined: "The time we enjoy wasting is not wasted time," "Before you kill a snake think hantavirus," and "There will be no work in heaven no one is going to screw it up."

As time went by, he grew more whimsical and erected elaborate folk art creations, such as a stump-and-bone tree (with the saying "Tree planted by Dooby, please don't pick the fruit") and a tribute to Elvis Presley. He built a small structure that has old television screens

On Doobie's road are many quips and phrases that make you think about the issues he raises.

Photo courtesy of the Nevada Commission on Tourism

for windows and named it the "Desert Broadcasting System." Other exhibits addressed weightier issues, such as nuclear weapons and the Vietnam War. Williams had served in Japan in the weeks following the dropping of the atomic bomb and created *Ground Zero,* a depiction of an atomic bomb blast made of different-colored rocks. He wanted it to serve as a reminder that such things should never happen again.

In 2005 a rock slide covered a large portion of Guru Road, but much of the site has been restored with the help of the Friends of Black Rock/High Rock and other volunteers, who conduct a Guru Road Restoration effort each June.

One Man's Trash Is Another Man's Art

Imlay

Travelers on I-80, between Lovelock and Winnemucca, often wonder about the bizarre, three-story concrete-and-glass structure that sits near the Imlay exit. Known as *Thunder Mountain Monument,* it is the work of a self-taught environmental artist named Frank Van Zandt, who often called himself Chief Rolling Mountain Thunder. Born in Oklahoma in 1911, Van Zandt knocked around northern California for many years before arriving in Nevada in 1968. According to writer David W. Toll, who met Van Zandt in 1975, the artist was a divinity school dropout who had worked for two decades as a deputy sheriff in Sutter County, California, and later as a private investigator.

In the mid-1960s Van Zandt's truck broke down near the former railroad siding in Imlay. He pushed it over to a spot beside the road and began living with his wife in the truck. According to Toll, the property's owner offered to sell Van Zandt the five-acre property at a bargain, so he bought it. Later press accounts reported that Van Zandt said that he had a vision telling him to move to the site, which is located in the shadow of Thunder Mountain. He purportedly believed that the area had special spiritual qualities.

Once entrenched on his land, he embraced a 1960s version of a traditional Native American lifestyle—he said in several interviews that he had Creek and Cheyenne Indian blood—and operated a school at which he taught the fundamentals of how to live like a Native American. He also began work on his creation. Difficult to describe—and equally difficult to miss from the freeway—*Thunder Mountain* is without a doubt one of the most unusual pieces of folk art in Nevada.

To understand *Thunder Mountain,* you have to envision similar folk art projects, such as the famed *Watts Towers* in southern California. Van Zandt erected the monument between 1969 and 1972, using whatever materials he could find because he said nothing should ever be wasted. As a result, the monument is constructed of discarded tools, old bottles, auto parts, windshields, wood scraps, railroad

***Thunder Mountain*—where one man's junk became another man's artwork.**

ties, and other found objects. The structure is a conglomeration of weird stairways and ladders, spires, windows (many are old car windshields), arches, car axles, animal bones, bicycle parts, statues, and more. The artist also incorporated more than 200 sculptures of faces and small human figures (many with outstretched arms) into walls, doorjambs, surrounding trees, and other places.

Originally, the monument was larger, consisting of eight separate buildings, including a hostel, his studio, and a general store. In 1983, however, a mysterious fire destroyed five of the structures, which Van Zandt never rebuilt. In 1992 *Thunder Mountain* was listed on the Nevada State Register of Historic Places. It is still owned by members of his family and is open to the public. The artist, who committed suicide in 1989, said that the purpose of his monument was to celebrate the people who had come before him, particularly Native Americans. "It's not a put-down, it's my monument, a dedication to all those people who came before us," he told the Associated Press in 1976.

What's in a Name?

Jiggs

Not many places can boast that they were named after a comic strip character. The settlement of Jiggs, Nevada, however, not only can make that claim but also holds the dubious record for changing its name almost as many times as Michael Jackson has had plastic surgery.

The first non-Indian settler in the area was W. M. Kennedy, who established a small spread there in 1866 and named the region Mound Valley (the largest landmarks were two large mounds). Three years later, David E. Hooten, who had unsuccessfully mined in Virginia City, erected a way station on a new toll road through the valley and named it—surprise—Hooten Station. A nearby ranch became the area's first post office, which was named Cottonwood. Shortly after, that post office closed, and another one, called Dry Creek, was established. Still later, the post office was relocated, and the name was changed again to Mound Valley.

In 1884 a new post office named Skelton opened. This moniker stuck around until 1911, when merchant John Jesse Hylton petitioned to change the name to Hylton. In 1918 Hylton, who owned most of the community's businesses, sold his holdings to Albert Hankins. Not wanting to continue using the previous owner's name for his town, Hankins listened when his children badgered him to name the town Jiggs, after one of their favorite comic strip characters (in the then-popular strip *Bringing Up Father*). Some historians have suggested that the children picked the name because the comic strip character Jiggs was always fighting with his wife, Maggie, in the same manner that the town could never agree on a name. On December 18, 1918, the town was renamed Jiggs. The name has stuck around for the past nine decades, so it appears this one is a keeper.

The best place to hear about Jiggs's identity crisis is probably the Jiggs Bar, a small local watering hole in the center of the tiny hamlet, which is located about 30 miles south of Elko via Routes 227 and 228. If you stop into the bar, be sure to check out the bizarre, two-headed calf mounted on the wall. If that doesn't make you want to have a drink, nothing will.

A True Circuit Court

Lovelock

There's an old joke told about the unusual round-shaped Pershing County Courthouse in Lovelock, which is 93 miles east of Reno. According to the story, a bickering couple went there to get a divorce—and they've been going round and round about it ever since.

The courthouse's circular footprint was the work of Reno architect Frederick J. DeLongchamps, who designed no fewer than seven courthouses in Nevada between 1911 and 1922. The structure, one of only two round courthouses in the United States (the other is a modern glass structure in San Antonio, Texas), incorporates a classical revival style of architecture and was patterned after the Pantheon in Rome. Constructed between 1919 and 1920, it remains in use.

The main courtroom, in the center of the building, has a theater-

Lovelock's Love Locks

Despite its romantic-sounding appellation, the town of Lovelock was actually named for a nineteenth-century cattleman, George Lovelock, who in 1869 donated the land for a train depot and the town site. That fact, however, hasn't stopped Lovelock from being a popular place for some couples to tie the knot. In the 1990s actor Kelsey Grammer (of *Frasier* fame) was married in Lovelock because he and his bride-to-be liked the town's name. On Valentine's Day 2006 the community even embraced an ancient Chinese custom and began urging visitors to "Lock Your Love in Lovelock." According to the tradition, couples symbolically lock their love for each other by attaching locks onto a chain. The legend is that love will endure as long as the lock remains on the chain.

As one of only ten U.S. communities with the word "love" in its name (according to the U.S. Census), Lovelock decided to take advantage of the custom and built the Lovers Lock Plaza on the grounds of the Pershing County Courthouse. The plaza contains sections of chain attached to concrete pillars that surround a small garden area. Visitors attach their own "love locks" to the chain links—and thousands have done so. The Chinese "love lock" tradition apparently has been around for many years, although no one is certain how or when it was started. In the Yellow Mountains of China, miles of lock-laden chains stretch across the landscape.

Couples interested in permanently locking their love in Lovelock can contact the office of the local justice of the peace, located inside the round courthouse, or call (775) 273-2753.

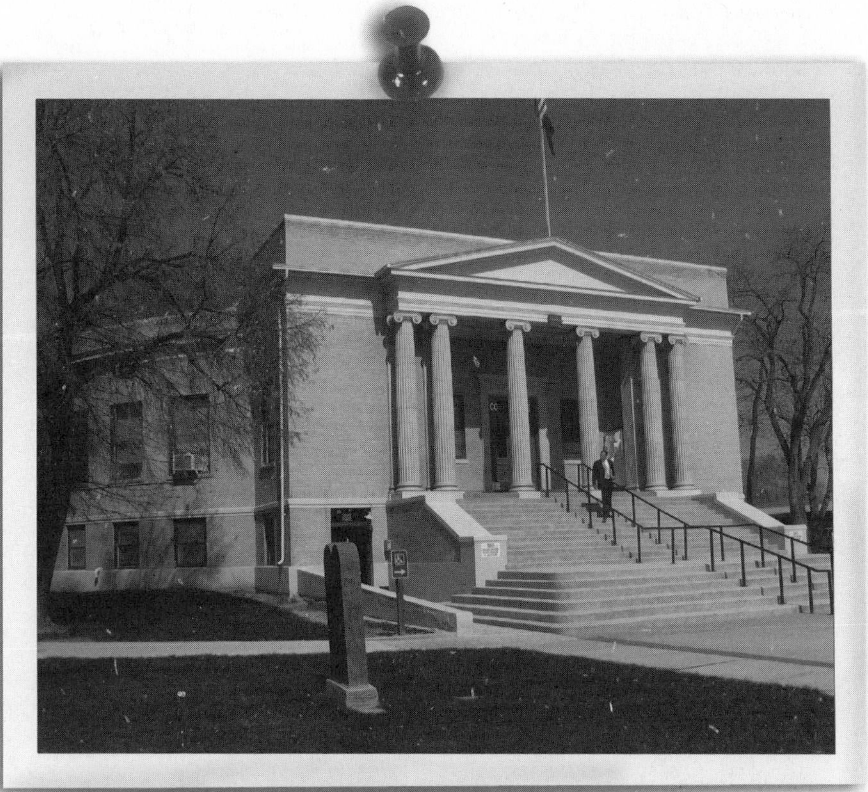

For years, divorcing couples have been going round and round at the Pershing County Courthouse in Lovelock.

in-the-round configuration. Courthouse staff members note that the round shape creates "dead spots" in the room where it can be difficult to hear what is being said by jurors, witnesses, or attorneys. In other places, however, the acoustics are so sensitive that a whisper can be heard on the opposite side of the room.

In the building's basement is a small display featuring local legal history. The exhibit is open Monday through Friday, 8:00 a.m. to 5:00 p.m., and there is no admission fee. The Pershing County Courthouse is located at 400 Main Street in Lovelock. For more information call (775) 273-7144.

Getting Away from It All

Tuscarora

When ceramic artist Dennis Parks decided to escape from the stifling world of academia in 1972, he probably couldn't have found a place much more remote than Tuscarora, Nevada. Parks was a promising young art professor in southern California living the traditional American dream with a wife, two sons, and a mortgage. A few years earlier, a friend had introduced him to the peace and quiet of Tuscarora, a decaying mining town about 55 miles north of Elko. Finding that the area had excellent clay soil for pottery and instantly attracted

Artist Dennis Parks found his muse in the old mining town of Tuscarora.

to the locale's slow pace of life and magnificent high desert scenery, Parks opened a seasonal school and studio. Feeling stressed out by the southern California lifestyle and wanting to raise his children away from the big-city environment—at least for a short time—he and his wife, Julie, originally planned to spend about a year in Tuscarora before returning to Los Angeles.

Once there, he acquired an old hotel, which he transformed into the Tuscarora School of Pottery (P.O. Box 6, Tuscarora, NV 89834; 775-756-5526; www.tuscarorapottery.com), while his wife became the town's postmaster. The school quickly gained an international reputation, and students began arriving from all over the world. The year in Tuscarora became two years, then several decades. As he notes in his autobiography, *Living in the Country Growing Weird: A Deep Rural Adventure,* over time he and his family evolved from big-city folk to rural people, and along the way they learned how to raise farm animals, plant gardens, fight crickets, and survive all the other challenges of rural Nevada. In fact, the Parks family came to love their community so much that they led a successful effort to fight off a mining company that wanted to move the historic mining town in order to develop a huge open-pit mine on the site.

These days, Dennis Parks is retired but still putters around the school. His son, Ben, a noted artist in his own right, does all the teaching, while Julie Parks is still the postmaster and operates the local library. It doesn't look like they're going to be returning to southern California.

Virgin Valley's Famous Fire Opals

Virgin Valley

Not all of the world's most famous jewels or stones can be found on the fingers of cocktail waitresses in Las Vegas. In fact, the world's best-known black fire opal was discovered in the remote Virgin Valley, 135 miles northwest of Winnemucca, in 1917. The 2,610-carat stone, which weighs one and a half pounds, was uncovered at the

Visitors can search for opals-in-the-rough at one of the do-it-yourself opal mines in Nevada's Virgin Valley.

Rainbow Ridge Mine and sold to Colonel W. A. Roebling, a world-famous collector of rare gems and rocks—and the civil engineer who helped design and build the Brooklyn Bridge in New York. Roebling later donated the stone to the Smithsonian Institution, where it remains on display in the Gem Hall.

Trivia

Wendover's Historic Graffiti

At the start of World War II, the U.S. military opened the Wendover Bombing and Gunnery Range in the desert flats outside Wendover. Over the next several years, the facility expanded as additional companies of troops were sent there for training. In 1944 Wendover was selected to be the training ground for the 509th Composite Group, a top-secret contingent of troops that trained and prepared to drop an atomic bomb on Japan. On August 6, 1945, the group's commander, Colonel Paul Tibbets Jr., piloted the *Enola Gay,* which dropped such a device on Hiroshima, Japan, effectively ending the war.

During their time in Wendover, bored airmen and soldiers began painting the giant rocks and cliffs overlooking the area with messages and images, including the numerical insignias of the various troop companies. The graffiti has long been considered an eyesore, but in recent years historians have begun to view the painted white letters and drawings as an important snapshot of that era.

The graffiti on the rocks above Wendover is actually considered historic, with much of it dating back to World War II.

The rare black fire opal, which is Nevada's official state precious gemstone, is a dark but translucent opal that, when held in the light, displays bright flashes of red coloring. Nevada's Virgin Valley is renowned for its opals, which include not only the rare black fire opal but also a wide variety of other opals. Geologists trace the origins of the region's opals back to one of Nevada's violent volcanic periods, which occurred about twenty million years ago. During that time of great upheaval, a basin was formed in the area. Over the years the basin filled with sediments and volcanic ash as well as deposits of silica. Eventually, forests in the basin were buried beneath the layers of sediment. The valley's opals essentially were created by the combination of warm underground water, silica deposits, and buried wood. Over time this geologic cocktail developed into opalized wood as well as opal stones.

Since the early twentieth century, miners have been working the Virgin Valley ground for opals. At Rainbow Ridge (where the Roebling opal was discovered) and several other commercial dig-it-yourself mines, rock hounds pay a fee for the right to sift through piles of dirt and rock, searching for anything that looks shiny and valuable. And who knows—maybe one of them will find the next Roebling opal.

For more information about fee mining for opals, go to www.nevadaopal.com (for Rainbow Ridge), www.royalpeacock.com (Royal Peacock Mine), or www.bonanzaopals.com (Bonanza Opal Mine).

Butch Cassidy Robbery

Winnemucca

One of the most cherished legends in Winnemucca is about the time Butch Cassidy and the Sundance Kid rode into town and robbed the local bank. Following the success of the 1969 movie *Butch Cassidy and the Sundance Kid,* the town began celebrating Butch Cassidy Days, which included a reenactment of the shootout at the First National Bank. According to the story, on September 19, 1900, the notorious Hole-in-the-Wall Gang, which included Butch (real name:

Robert Leroy Parker) and Sundance (real name: Harry Longabaugh), rode into Winnemucca and stole $32,000 in gold from the bank. Later, Butch allegedly sent the bank a photograph of himself and the gang, along with a thank-you note for the money.

Unfortunately, the tale is only partially true. There was a robbery on that date, and it appears that members of the Hole-in-the-Wall Gang participated, perhaps including the Sundance Kid, but the rest of the story is hokum. Historical investigators have placed Butch in Tipton, Wyoming, on the day of the robbery, and an eyewitness could not identify him as having been at the scene of the crime. Even the story about the photograph and the thank-you note is either a concoction or at least a misunderstanding. Historical records indicate that the Pinkerton Detective Agency, which was trying to capture the gang, sent the picture to the bank's president so that he could use it to identify which members had taken part in the theft. He failed to spot either Butch Cassidy or the Sundance Kid as having been in his bank that day, but the Pinkerton Agency still offered a reward for the arrest of either for the robbery.

No one was ever arrested for the Winnemucca robbery—which only adds to the mystery. As for Butch and Sundance, in February 1902 the duo, along with Butch's common-law wife, Etta Place, sailed from New York to Buenos Aires, Argentina. They tried ranching for a few years before slipping back into their previous roles as bank robbers. They were reportedly killed in Bolivia in February 1908.

The First National Bank of Winnemucca is no longer in business, but the building where the robbery took place is still there, on the corner of Fourth and Bridge Streets in downtown Winnemucca. Across the street there's a restaurant called Butch Cassidy's Hole-in-the-Wall (233 South Bridge Street), proving that the legend lives on.

CHAPTER

7

Reno–Lake Tahoe

Cradle of Nevada

"Reno sits here upon a river-meadow with her back against the High Sierra and her face toward the Great Desert—and does not care what people say of her."

—Max Miller, *Reno* (1941)

Long before Las Vegas *had become synonymous with sin, Reno was America's favorite bad-boy city. In the early twentieth century, Reno capitalized on Nevada's lax divorce laws and became famous as the place to quickly and easily untie the bonds of matrimony, a process known as "the Cure." It was also a place where gambling could be found, even before it was fully legalized in Nevada, and the alcohol flowed pretty freely, even during Prohibition. In fact, one 1930s mayor, E. E. Roberts, suggested that "the only way to put bootleggers out of business is to place a barrel of good corn whiskey on every downtown street corner, with dipper attached, and signs inviting passersby to help themselves to all they want, free of charge."*

The circumstances surrounding Reno's birth might partially explain the city's "whatever" attitude. Essentially, it was a railroad and banking center that catered to the get-rich-fast miners in nearby Virginia City. Reno was never a mining town, but it did depend on mining towns, which, naturally, affected its overall outlook as a wide-open town. So even though Reno ain't Vegas, it also isn't Bedford Falls. Thank goodness.

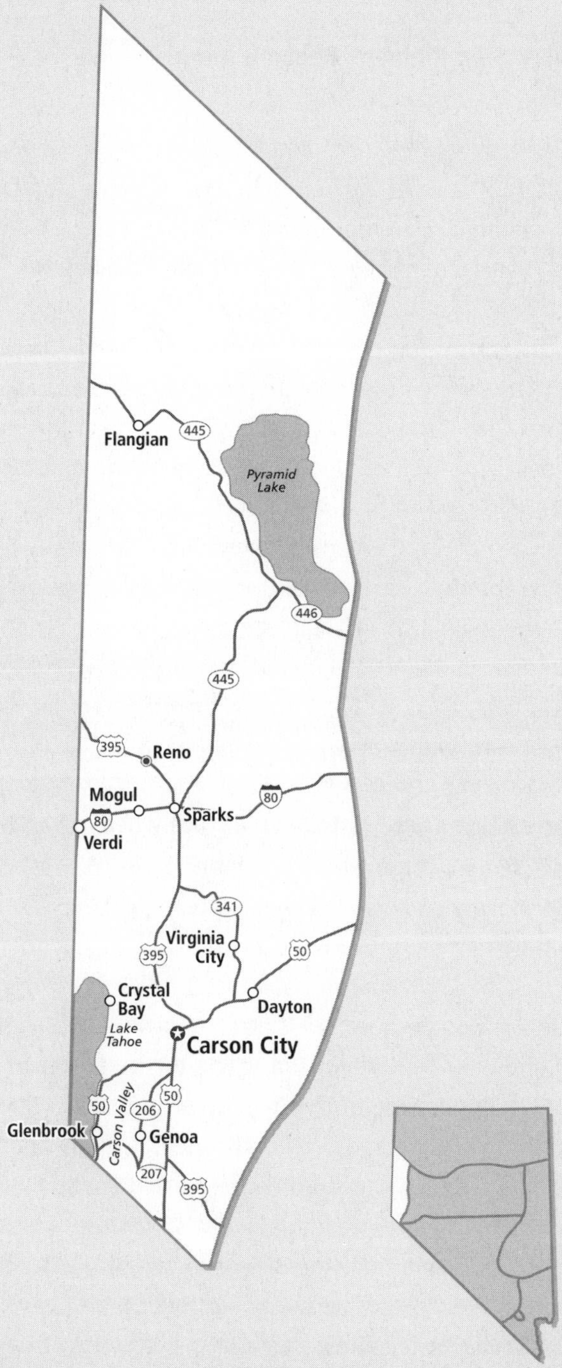
Flangian
445
Pyramid Lake
446
445
395
Reno
Mogul
80
Sparks
80
Verdi
341
Virginia City
395
50
Crystal Bay
Dayton
Lake Tahoe
Carson City
50
50
206
Carson Valley
Glenbrook
Genoa
207
395

Reno-Tahoe

Where Sam Clemens Became Mark Twain

Carson City

In 1861 Samuel Clemens and his older brother, Orion, arrived in Carson City. The elder Clemens had been hired as secretary to Nevada's new territorial governor, James W. Nye. Samuel Clemens, then twenty-six years old, had worked as a printer, a typesetter, and a steamboat pilot (and had deserted a Confederate militia) before joining his brother on the journey to the American West.

After arriving in Carson City, Sam Clemens embarked on a quest to make his fortune and visited various parts of the state, including Unionville, as well as California, where he tried his hand at mining, stock trading, and other unsuccessful endeavors. While in the mining camp of Aurora, Clemens began writing letters to Virginia City's *Territorial Enterprise* newspaper using the pen name Josh. The witty letters about life at the mining camp caught the attention of the editor, who offered Clemens a job at the paper.

On February 3, 1863, Clemens signed one of his dispatches from Carson City with a new nom de plume, Mark Twain. According to Nevada author George Williams III, "'Mark Twain' was not born in Missouri as most of us have been taught. Mark Twain, the writer, the character, was born amidst the bitter odors of whisky, gin and beer in John Piper's saloon in Virginia City, Nevada." Williams writes that, contrary to the popular notion that Sam Clemens took the name because of a riverboat measurement, he acquired this nickname in Piper's saloon because of his habit of buying two drinks (one for himself and one for a friend) and telling the bartender to "mark twain" on his tab, meaning to charge him for two drinks. Williams believes that in his later years Clemens changed the story about how he adopted the pen name in order to make it sound more respectable.

During his tenure at the *Territorial Enterprise,* Clemens utilized his gift for satire, crafting stories—regardless of the truth—that would amuse his readers, while tweaking the rich, the powerful, or the foolish. In 1863 he began his career as a humorist with a lecture to benefit the construction of the First Presbyterian Church in Carson City (110 North Nevada Street).

In 1864 Clemens, by now known as Mark Twain, departed Virginia City for San Francisco (apparently, he became party to a proposed duel and felt that discretion was the better part of valor). There, he wrote for the *Morning Call* newspaper, then for the *Californian,* a literary magazine. Twain returned to Nevada twice, in 1866 and in 1868 (after he had traveled to Hawaii, which he would write about in his book *Innocents Abroad*), as a lecturer. After 1868, however, Twain never again visited the West. His brother's home (502 North Division Street) in Carson City is still standing.

And while Twain once famously said that reports of his death were greatly exaggerated, his beloved niece, Jennie Clemens, who died of spotted fever in 1864 at the age of nine, is buried in Carson City's Lone Mountain Cemetery. For those who dig cemeteries—as the French do—Lone Mountain Cemetery is located at 1044 Beverly Drive in the northern part of Carson City. From Reno, head south on US 395 for about 25 miles; then go west on East College Parkway to North Roop Street. Continue for a few miles on Roop, which intersects with Beverly.

And It All Started in Carson City

Carson City

Nevada has long hosted championship boxing matches, mostly in Las Vegas. But few know that the first major legal professional boxing bout occurred in Carson City in 1897. The match was between heavyweight champ "Gentleman" Jim Corbett and challenger Bob Fitzsimmons, the New Zealand heavyweight champion. The bout, which attracted 4,000 onlookers, generated considerable publicity for the state of Nevada, largely because it was the first championship fight ever filmed for later public exhibition in theaters.

The fight, which Fitzsimmons won, was the start of Nevada's successful partnership with boxing. Prior to the Corbett-Fitzsimmons fight, professional boxing was illegal in Nevada. In 1897, in order to land the Corbett-Fitzsimmons match, the Nevada state legislature voted to legalize boxing, thus ushering in a new era.

Today, dozens of prizefights are held each year throughout the state, with the bulk of them in Las Vegas. In recent years Nevada has hosted many of the highest-grossing (live gate) championship fights, including Lennox Lewis versus Evander Holyfield in 1999, Mike Tyson versus Holyfield in 1996, and Oscar De La Hoya versus Floyd Mayweather Jr. in 2007. Among the more noteworthy fights to take place in the state have been the 1985 Marvin Hagler–Thomas Hearns fight, which many boxing historians think is one of the greatest middleweight bouts of all time, and the infamous Tyson–Holyfield fight in 1997 (the "Bite of the Century"), during which Tyson was disqualified after biting off a piece of Holyfield's ear.

For a full schedule of Nevada boxing events, go to the Web site of the Nevada State Athletic Commission at http://boxing.nv.gov/schedule.htm.

In the Footprints of Prehistoric Giants

Carson City

In the late 1870s inmates at the Nevada State Prison were cutting sandstone at the prison quarry when they uncovered animal tracks and a trail of large footprints in the rock. The footprints were particularly noteworthy because they appeared to be human and measured an amazing 19 inches long and 8 inches wide. In 1882 Storey County sheriff W. J. Hanks asked H. W. Harkness of the California Academy of Sciences in San Francisco to investigate. A team of experts from the academy studied the tracks, and several of the scientists concluded that the footprints were indeed made by giant humans because they curved like a human foot. Furthermore, they said that the giants were wearing huge sandals, which explained the enormous size of the imprints.

According to Eugene M. Hattori, Curator of Anthropology at the Nevada State Museum, there were discrepancies that the scientists couldn't explain. For example, Hattori notes that "the left and right footprints were spread over 18 inches apart, a much wider span than expected for even giant humans." Hattori said another scientist, Professor Joseph LeConte, viewed the tracks and came to a different conclusion—that most likely they were made by a large quadruped, such as a prehistoric giant ground sloth. His argument was bolstered by the fact that bones of a giant sloth species known as *Mylodon* had been found in the same quarry.

Even humorist Mark Twain, who had spent several years in Nevada, was compelled to comment. In 1884 he wrote that he had been there when the tracks had been formed. He said they "were made by the first Nevada Territorial Legislature," which he had covered when they met at a hotel near the site where the prison was located.

"It had rained all the evening outside, and it had whiskey all the evening inside," Twain explained. He said that the legislators, led by the Speaker, had stepped in the mud and made the large footprints, and the reason they were heading north was because that was the direction of the saloons. "Such is history. Such are the Carson Foot-prints. They are not fossiliferous, they are legislative," he added.

The controversy simmered for several decades until paleontologist Chester Stock of the University of California, who excavated the Rancho La Brea tar pits in southern California, studied the prints and concluded that they were identical to sloth prints found at La Brea. In 1917 Stock crafted a reconstruction of the giant ground sloth's foot and matched its imprint with the Carson Prison prints, thereby ending the mystery.

If you're interested in viewing the giant prints, a reconstruction of a print is displayed in the geology gallery at the Nevada State Museum, 600 North Carson Street in Carson City (about 25 miles south of Reno via US 395), and a few of the actual footprints cut from the bedrock are displayed in the Keck Museum in the Mackay School of Mines building on the University of Nevada–Reno campus.

The Man Who Created the One-Armed Bandit

Carson City

The next time you pop a quarter into a slot machine and watch it disappear faster than dessert at a Reno buffet, blame it on Charles August Fey. Born in Bavaria in 1862, Fey immigrated to San Francisco in 1885 and went to work for an electrical company as an instrument maker. In 1894 he and a coworker opened Holtz and Fey Electric Works, and Fey began working in the basement of his apartment on a mechanical gambling machine. Later that year, he created the Horseshoe, an early version of a slot machine, followed by the 4-11-44, another slot-type game of chance that proved successful. In 1896 he opened his own factory. Two years later, he developed the Card Bell, a three-wheel, staggered-stop slot machine with an automatic coin payout design—a precursor to the modern slot machine. In 1899 he refined the machine by changing the images on the reels from playing card designs to symbols such as stars and bells. This new version, the Liberty Bell, was enormously popular and became the standard for the burgeoning slot machine industry.

Other manufacturers soon began to copy Fey's design—patent laws did not apply to gambling devices—although that didn't stop him from continuing to produce slot machines. Until his death in 1944, Fey manufactured dozens of different gaming devices, including the Silver Cup, featuring two spinning wheels; the Rock-A-Way, which featured two girls on a teeter-totter that rocked back and forth as the nickel dropped through the playing field; and Skill-Draw, a mechanical poker device.

Fey's direct connection to Nevada began in 1958, when two of his grandsons, Marshall and Franklin Fey, moved to Reno to open the Liberty Belle Restaurant and Saloon at 4250 South Virginia. Over the years the two filled the establishment, known for its prime rib and steaks, with old-time antiques, such as an elaborate back-bar, ornate nineteenth-century brass cash registers, elegant antique chandeliers, historic posters, and, of course, vintage slot machines. Over time

Photo courtesy of Scott Klette/Nevada State Museum

The machine that emptied a million pockets—the Liberty Bell slot machine

Marsh Fey acquired nearly 200 historic mechanical gaming devices, assembling one of the finest private collections of antique slots. Among the machines contained in the Fey collection were two original Liberty Bell units (only seven are thought to still exist). A few of the best Fey devices (as well as antique machines built by his contemporaries) were displayed in the restaurant, but the bulk of the collection was crammed in an attic above part of the restaurant that wasn't open to the public (although the Feys occasionally opened it for private tours). Marsh Fey has authored a pictorial history of the slot machine, originally to highlight his grandfather's role in its invention; the book is currently in its sixth edition, with more than 33,000 copies sold.

In early 2007 the Fey brothers, both in their seventies and faced with the expensive prospect of replacing the restaurant's roof, closed the venerable Reno landmark, announced they were going to auction its antiques, and sold the site to the adjacent Reno-Sparks Convention Center for a parking lot. Fortunately, the two brothers also indicated that they would be willing to sell the most historically significant machines in the collection, all made by Charles Fey between 1895 and 1937, to the State of Nevada. To give the state time to raise funds for the purchase, they loaned the twenty-five devices to the Nevada State Museum for a one-year show.

In June 2007 the Nevada state legislature appropriated funds to buy the two dozen machines and make them a permanent part of the State Museum's collection. To see these ornate, vintage slot machines, visit the State Museum, 600 North Carson Street, Carson City.

Where Eagles Dare to Dine

Carson Valley

Discovering what majestic bald eagles like to eat is a bit like finding out what's inside a hot dog—it's probably best not to think about it too much. Every February, dozens of bald eagles flock to the Carson Valley, south of Reno, to feed on one of their favorite snacks: nutrient-rich afterbirths of newborn calves. Strangely enough, viewing these marvelous birds as they feast on fetal leftovers is a lot more appealing than it sounds.

This symbiotic relationship between bird and cow has occurred for a long time, but only in recent years have tourists discovered the phenomenon. In fact, since 2002 the Carson Valley Visitors Authority has organized formal eco-friendly tours of various area ranches, at which onlookers can catch a glimpse or snap a photo of one of those mighty raptors. The Eagles and Agriculture Event attracts an estimated 700 eagle-eyed bird-watchers each year.

Many people simply park by the side of the road to view the magnificent birds feasting in the birthing pastures; however, those paying to take the official tour (about $50) pile into luxury buses and are whisked off to local ranches to look at bald eagles as well as golden eagles, red-tailed hawks, marsh hawks, owls, and kestrels. Birding specialists lead the tours and describe raptor migration, the biology of birds of prey, and habitat. In addition to the eagle tours, the event includes presentations by visiting avian experts, an evening Owl Prowl, a photography workshop, and a guided raft-canoe trip on the Carson River to observe various birds. For information about the event, contact the Carson Valley Visitors Authority (800-727-7677; www.visitcarsonvalley.org).

Crazy George's Cool Pad

Crystal Bay

George Whittell Jr. was a true party animal—and he had a deep fondness for both. In the 1930s and 1940s, Whittell, a wealthy San Francisco businessman, indulged his twin passions at his Lake Tahoe summer mansion, called the Thunderbird Lodge, by hosting legendary all-night poker and drinking parties and maintaining a small, personal zoo at his estate, which grew to include a pet lion and an elephant. Today, the nonprofit Thunderbird Lodge Preservation Society manages Whittell's marvelous Tudor revival hideaway on behalf of the U.S. Forest Service, which owns the property. Group tours are available by reservation (www.thunderbirdlodge.org).

The estate offers a glimpse into Whittell's world. The lodge is an almost perfect blending of architectural design with the natural environment. The lodge's stone-and-wood exterior seems organic—as if it belongs alongside the surrounding giant granite boulders and thick stands of conifers. The six-acre compound includes a large, stone main house with two master bedrooms, three smaller bedrooms, and a great room with a full-size movie screen.

Whittell also built the Card House, a separate stone structure where he and his pals could play cards, smoke cigars, and, it is said, enjoy female companionship. Adjacent is the Boat House, a long, narrow one-story structure at lake level that houses his 55-foot-long mahogany speedboat called, appropriately, *Thunderbird*. A secret, 600-foot-long tunnel, blasted through solid granite, connects the Card House and the Boat House to the lodge (and, according to rumor, allowed Whittell to surreptitiously bring in women for his parties).

Whittell was born into a wealthy San Francisco family in 1881. After graduating from high school, he skipped college and joined the Barnum and Bailey Circus, where he developed a lifelong interest in exotic animals. After a few years Whittell returned to San Francisco to resume his life as a social dilettante. Following two brief marriages—to a chorus girl and a singer—he became an ambulance driver during World War I. He was slightly wounded and ended up in a French hospital, where he fell in love with his nurse, Elia Pascal. They subsequently married. Following his father's death in 1922, Whittell inherited $30 million.

In the early 1930s Whittell moved to Nevada in order to avoid California's taxes. He purchased more than 40,000 acres of land on the Nevada side of Lake Tahoe, which included about 27 miles of shoreline. In 1937 he began construction of the Thunderbird Lodge. Whittell's personal zoo started with a pet lion cub given to him as a gift. Named Bill, the lion became Whittell's constant companion, riding with him in the car (Whittell owned six Duesenbergs). Over time Whittell added a pet elephant as well as other lions and more than forty birds.

Just prior to his death in 1969, Whittell sold a portion of his immense land holdings to the National Forest Service and the State of Nevada for public use. In 1972 the Thunderbird Lodge was sold to New York financier Jack Dreyfus, who added another master bedroom and an entertainment room. In 1998 the Del Webb Corporation purchased the lodge and surrounding 140 acres for $50 million. A year later, Del Webb exchanged the property for surplus Bureau of Land Management land in southern Nevada.

The Many Legends of "Old Virginny"

Dayton

One of Nevada's most endearing legends is the story of "Old Virginny," the man considered one of the founders of the famous Nevada mining town of Virginia City. According to the oft-repeated

Final resting place of "Old Virginny"

story, late one night Old Virginny was walking down the muddy main street of the just-birthed mining camp in western Nevada when he stumbled, broke a bottle of whiskey he was carrying, and decided to christen the town Virginia City (or, in some versions, Virginia Town), in honor of his home state of Virginia.

Most historians, however, consider the story apocryphal. In his book *The Roar and the Silence,* Nevada State Historic Preservation Officer Ronald James expresses doubts about its authenticity and notes, "Evidence clearly indicates that local miners decided in a meeting to name the community Virginia City." James adds, however, that it is likely that the town name honored Old Virginny, who was a respected member of the community and one of the first miners to work in the area.

Moreover, there is some confusion about Old Virginny's actual name. In some books his name is given as James Finney, whereas in others it is James Fennimore (his tombstone in Dayton, Nevada, lists James Finney). According to historian Guy Rocha, Comstock journalist Dan DeQuille wrote that Old Virginny's real name was James Fennimore but that he changed it to James Finney when he came to Nevada in 1851 because he thought he had killed a man in California. Rocha also notes that in Myron Angel's *History of Nevada* (1881), Fennimore's name is spelled "Fenimore" and his nickname is "Old Virginia."

And then there are the variations in the stories about his death. According to Rocha, Charles H. Lincoln wrote that on about April 26, 1861, he stopped at an old adobe hotel in Dayton, Nevada; tied his horse outside; and went inside for dinner. While Lincoln was still inside, Fennimore untied the horse, climbed onto the animal, but was thrown from the saddle before he had ridden very far. He died the next day from injuries suffered as a result of the fall and was buried in Dayton. However, Eliot Lord writes in his book *Comstock Mining and Miners* (1883) that Fennimore fell from his own horse, fractured his skull, and died on June 20, 1861. DeQuille places the death in

July 1861 and writes that Fennimore had been thrown from a bucking mustang he had been trying to ride while "under the influence of liquor."

Ron James notes it took less than two decades for the legends about Fennimore/Finney to take root. He observes that in these tales, hardworking, serious miners were transformed into eccentric, devil-may-care drunks because "the latter fit easily into the legendary Wild West during its carefree frontier period; the former would contradict that image."

James adds, "Ultimately, the story of the discovery of the Comstock Lode illustrates the power of the myth of the Wild West and exemplifies how quickly it could claim the imagination."

Of course, if you want to ask him yourself, you can visit Old Virginny in the Dayton Cemetery, located on a hillside directly west of the old mining town of Dayton. Dayton is about 43 miles southeast of Reno via US 395 and US 50.

The Oldest Thirst Parlor in the State

Genoa

Besides claiming to be the oldest permanent settlement in Nevada, Genoa also boasts of having the oldest saloon in the state. This venerable drinking establishment is known as the Old Genoa Bar (2282 Main Street), and it traces its roots to 1863, when the brick structure was built as Livingston's Exchange. In 1884 the building was purchased by Frank Fettic, who renamed it Fettic's Exchange and publicly operated it as a "Gentleman's Saloon." Since then, it has continuously functioned as a purveyor of adult spirits.

David W. Toll, author of *The Complete Nevada Traveler,* notes that like a lot of claims involving being first, the Old Genoa Bar has had challenges. For instance, several years ago the Delta Saloon in Virginia City announced that it had been operating since 1860 and therefore was the oldest saloon in the state. But historians noted that the Delta had moved at least once since it opened, so it couldn't back up the claim.

The Old Genoa Bar claims to be the state's oldest "thirst parlor."

A trip to the Old Genoa Bar is a chance to step into the past. The walls are cluttered with old posters, political campaign flyers, mounted deer heads, and newspaper clippings. The floor is uneven, the pool table is worn, a couple of small wooden tables and chairs are scattered about, and a wood-burning stove stands in a corner. Old-fashioned oil lamps hang from the ceiling, and the place looks as though it hasn't been dusted in more than a century. The rustic, frontier ambience has given the bar some street cred—it has appeared in several films. But it's got a kind of warm, friendly vibe, like a good neighborhood bar, and the beer is cold. No wonder it's managed to stay in business since 1863.

The Confectionery Ball

Genoa

In 1919 the tiny community of Genoa, one of Nevada's earliest settlements, wanted to purchase streetlights. Lacking a tax base, the citizens decided to hold a "Candy Dance" to raise money for the public illumination. Lillian Virgin Finnegan, daughter Judge Daniel Webster Virgin, a prominent figure in the community, suggested the dance as well as the idea of passing candy around during the affair. She believed that the free, homemade sweets would attract a better turnout. The event would also include a midnight dinner special at the Raycraft Hotel.

Genoa historian Billie Jean Rightmore notes that Finnegan and her aunt, Jane Raycraft Campbell, persuaded most of the women in Genoa to cook up the confections. The dance was a hit, with most folks particularly enjoying the delicious sweets. The community raised enough money to purchase the streetlights, but the town quickly realized that it needed some way to pay for the electricity to keep them operating. So it was decided to hold the Candy Dance each year, with the proceeds paying for a year's worth of electricity.

Since then, the dance and dinner have continued be held annually. In fact, the town, which has about 250 residents, sells 4,000 pounds of homemade fudge, divinity, and other tasty sweets, along with T-shirts and other food. In recent years the Candy Dance has generated $90,000 to $100,000 annually for the town, with the proceeds going toward community projects such as roads, park maintenance, storm drains, firefighting, and other civic services.

In the 1970s an arts and crafts fair was added to boost attendance. The first year, there were a dozen vendors, who set up booths on the front lawn of a private residence. Over the years the number of artisans has increased. Now the fair is held over two days, has about 350 exhibitor booths spread over the grounds of the Mormon Station Historic State Monument and the Genoa Town Park, and attracts more than 80,000 people.

The Genoa Candy Dance includes an arts and crafts fair and a candy sale to raise money for the town's services.

If you're interested in attending, the Candy Dance Arts and Crafts Faire is held the last full weekend in September. Hours are 9:00 a.m. to 5:00 p.m. The town of Genoa is located 48 miles south of Reno via US 395 and Route 206 (Genoa Lane). For more information call (775) 782-8696 or go to www.genoanevada.org/candydanceevent-days.htm.

Beware the Spirits of Cave Rock

Lake Tahoe

Once upon a time, Lake Tahoe's Cave Rock was actually a cave. Today, most people know Cave Rock only as a tunnel through the rocks on the east side of Lake Tahoe, but geologically speaking the cave is part of a 360-foot-high volcanic plug. The cave walls are andesite, while the surrounding cliffs are granite.

Cave Rock holds special significance for the native Washoe people who inhabited Lake Tahoe for centuries before the arrival of white European settlers. It's said that in the summer when tribal members would hunt, fish, and gather food around Lake Tahoe, their spiritual leaders would go to the cave to think and meditate. A U.S. Forest Service environmental report on Cave Rock described it as both an archaeological site and a historic transportation district. "It is also a sacred site to the Washoe Tribe of California and Nevada," the report noted. "Many members of the Washoe Tribe object to human presence at Cave Rock and believe that only special people, Washoe spiritual elders, should be there."

The first written record of this Tahoe landmark comes from the mid-1850s, when surveyor George H. Goddard described it as a "legendary cave." His description reflected the importance the cave had to the Washoe. According to one of the tribe's legends, the cave was formed by the Great Spirit after the waters of the lake began to rise and threatened to drown the Washoe who lived by the rock. The Great Spirit thrust his spear into the rock to form a cave into which the water could drain. Yet another legend has it that the Paiute Indians, traditional enemies of the peace-loving Washoe, tried to conquer and enslave the Washoe tribe. The "god of the world" came to the rescue of the Washoe by creating the cave and imprisoning the Paiutes inside. There, the evil ones were transformed into water demons that were afraid of the lake and can never leave. It is said that their cries and moans can sometimes be heard coming from the cave. The legend seems to reflect the fact that the cave was apparently the site of many fierce turf skirmishes between the Washoe and the Paiutes over who could fish and hunt at Lake Tahoe.

Of course, it's difficult to imagine what Cave Rock originally looked like because it was blasted into Cave Tunnel in the early twentieth century. That's when a 200-foot passage was dug through the back of the cave and a parallel tunnel was blasted through the adjacent rock. You can still see a portion of the original cave part of the tunnel in the rugged rock walls that constitute several hundred feet of the southbound or west tunnel.

Before the cave became a tunnel, a road, called Lake Bigler Toll Road, went around the cave on the lakeside. In the mid-1860s a 1-mile road costing some $40,000 was constructed on the west face. When it was built, this section was the most expensive stretch of road between Placerville and Washoe City. About 0.25 mile of the road remains visible, including hand-chiseled stone buttresses. At the westernmost point, where the road was apparently built out over the lake and was supported by a 100-foot trestle bridge (it collapsed long ago), the road is gone, and there is a steep drop-off to the rocks and water below.

Additionally, from the southern side, several smaller caves can be seen in the rock. One, located above the median between the northbound and southbound traffic lanes, is actually fairly large. It's said that if you listen hard, you can hear the wind whistling through it—or perhaps it's the faint wailing of those water demons. From the north side at the waterline, you can also see several shapes in the rock face below the tunnel that have been given names; for example, above the waterline is the 50-foot profile of the "Lady of the Lake" (complete with eyelashes), and located on the upper curve of the rock is the "Gorilla Profile." More recently, "Tahoe Tessie," a sea

Before it was turned into Cave Tunnel, Cave Rock was the source of many Washoe legends.

serpent–like monster, has allegedly been sighted at the lake in the waters below Cave Rock.

Cave Rock is one of the more popular boating and fishing spots of the Nevada Division of State Parks. Visitors will find a boat launch ramp, restrooms, and a pleasant, small sandy beach area with room for swimming or catching a few rays of sunlight. There is a day use fee for parking at Cave Rock and using the state park facilities. Cave Rock is located about 20 miles west of Carson City via US 50.

Mysterious Pyramid Lake

Pyramid Lake Paiute Reservation

Physical features define Pyramid Lake. The native Northern Paiute Indians, who have resided around that lake for centuries, called it "cu yui pah," which roughly translates as "lake of the cui-ui fish," after a species of fish in the lake that is sacred to the tribe. In 1844 explorer John C. Frémont came upon the desert lake's 125,000 acres of glistening water, which he said "broke upon our eyes like the ocean." He named it Pyramid Lake, after a 500-foot-high pyramid-shaped rock island that juts from the waters near the lake's southeastern shore.

Located about 30 miles north of Reno, Pyramid Lake has long been a special place for nearly everyone who has encountered it. In their tribal histories, the Northern Paiutes teach their children at an early age to respect the lake, which is part of the Pyramid Lake Paiute Reservation. "I used to tell my children, when you go to the lake, bless the water first. Wash your face with the water, then you can swim in the lake," said tribal member Mamie John in one of the tribal reports.

The lake's importance to the tribe is reflected in many myths and legends. The story about the creation of the lake's namesake pyramid rock is that it represents the spearhead of the Great Father, who is said to have thrust it upward from the earth to ward off a lengthy drought. The lake's shores are dotted with many interesting tufa formations—in fact, the pyramid is made of this pitted stone, which is formed when natural springs filled with calcium mineral water leak into salty, carbonate water. A chemical bonding occurs, which results in the creation of a limestone-like substance known as tufa. Formations such as those found around Pyramid Lake are the result of a buildup of tufa material, which can only occur underwater. However,

Photo courtesy of the Nevada Commission on Tourism

Mysterious Pyramid Lake, home of "water babies" and other legends

once water recedes and the tufa is exposed to air, it ceases to grow.

At several places along the shore, you can also find other unusual tufa formations. For instance, nearly adjacent to the pyramid are several giant tufa bubbles, which are mushroom-shaped rocks that are hollow in the middle. One of the most famous formations is "Great Stone Mother and Basket," a remarkable tufa shape that resembles a seated Indian woman with an open basket next to her. According to legend, some of Stone Mother's children were forced to move away because they couldn't get along with her other offspring. Stone Mother was so filled with remorse that she began to cry and filled the lake with her tears. Her basket remains empty, awaiting her children's return.

The lake is also said to be home to "water babies," which are powerful spirits that live in its waters. According to a 1934 article by Willard Z. Park on Paiute shamanism that appeared in *American Anthropologist,* "There are shamans who are visited in their dreams by the mythical beings living in the lakes and water holes and spoken of as 'water babies.' They are instructed in the same way as the other shamans and the water babies give them the songs that they are to use in curing. When anyone speaks skeptically of the water babies or makes fun of them, they are sure to hear and make the offender ill. Only a shaman with power obtained from the babies can cure such a case. The shaman is called in to treat the offender and he learns from his power what must be done to bring about recovery."

Some believe that the "water babies" at Pyramid Lake are mischievous and will pull at swimmers' legs. They claim that the spirits can drag a person into the lake, never to be seen again. Because the lake does have a strong undertow, there are occasional drownings. Moreover, the lake's depth—about 335 feet at its deepest—and cold water at the lower depths, keep the bodies of drowning victims from surfacing. Apparently, the cold water temperatures prevent the formation of gases that would normally cause a body to float to the surface.

Geologically speaking, Pyramid Lake is a remnant of an ancient inland sea, known as Lake Lahontan. Until about 12,000 years ago, this lake covered much of northern and central Nevada. Pyramid Lake receives most of its water from the Truckee River, which flows from

Snowshoe Thompson

One of the nearly forgotten figures in Nevada history is Jon Torsteinson Rui, better known as John "Snowshoe" Thompson. He is credited with introducing skiing to northern California and Nevada. Prior to his arrival in the region in the mid-1850s, no one had ever strapped on a pair of thin, wooden boards and slid down a hill.

Thompson was born in Norway in 1827. When he was ten years old, his family immigrated to America and settled in the Midwest. In 1851, however, John joined the thousands of people heading to California to mine for gold. Eventually, he was hired to carry mail between Placerville, California, and Genoa, Nevada. In order to make the trek in the winter, he crafted a pair of wooden skis, like the ones he had used as a boy in Norway. For the next two decades Thompson delivered the mail in small towns throughout the Sierra Nevada.

Over the years word spread about Thompson's "Norwegian snowshoes." He taught dozens of people how to glide across the snow and almost single-handedly introduced skiing to the region. Thompson died in 1876 and is buried in the quiet Genoa cemetery, which is located 15 miles southwest of Carson City via US 395 and Jack's Valley Road. The gravesite is at the rear of the cemetery, under large shade trees. Today, visitors can pay their respects to the father of Sierra Nevada skiing and view his unique tombstone, featuring the image of a pair of wooden skis carved into the white marble.

Grave of John "Snowshoe" Thompson, the man you can blame for snowboarders

Lake Tahoe. Among the fish that thrive in its waters is the rare cui-ui (pronounced "kwee-wee"), an endangered species that biologists believe has been around for more than two million years.

For more information about Pyramid Lake, contact the Pyramid Lake Museum and Visitor Center at (775) 574-1088.

Just beware of the "water babies."

Sheepherder Porn

Spooner Lake

The life of a nineteenth- or early-twentieth-century Nevada sheepherder could be lonely. It wasn't unusual for a sheep tender to watch over his flock for weeks or months alone in some remote mountain pasture or valley. Many of these young men hailed from the Basque territories of Spain and France, meaning they were far from home and friends and didn't understand English. To pass the time, some carved graffiti into the white bark of aspen trees. In some cases the carvings were little more than initials, dates, and nationalistic slogans, while others were more ribald or sexually suggestive.

Nevada has dozens of spots filled with this unique form of folk writing, known as arborglyphs, but one of the more accessible can be found in the groves of aspen trees on the slopes above Glenbrook, near Spooner Lake on the east side of Lake Tahoe. There, the grove and meadow once served as a summer range for Basque sheepherders and their flocks. If you wander through the Spooner aspen grove, you can find dozens of carvings made by Basque herders more than eighty years ago.

Some are humorous, such as a carved stick figure of a man sitting in front of a piano on what appears to be a toilet seat with the carved "E.M. 1932 . . . Playing the piano and . . ." A few trees away is another arborglyph, apparently by the same artist. It depicts a man riding on a horse. Dated August 21, 1932, the carving is detailed enough to reveal the rider's hat and scarf as well as a saddle, whip, and reins. Yet another arborglyph shows a fairly detailed representa-

Prior to the Internet, Basque sheepherders had tree porn.

tion of the flag of Spain, with the words "Espana, June 25, 1939," followed by writing (possibly Basque or Spanish words) that is difficult to decipher. Still others simply show carvings of men in striped shirts with cowboy hats.

Of course, because these young sheepherders were in the prime of their lives, they sometimes carved more sexually explicit images, such as a figure of a naked woman, sexual acts, and female anatomy. Basque history instructor Joxe Mallea-Olaetxe, who has studied the carvings, writes, "Anyone wanting to know what the world would be like without women need only become a sheepherder." He says that the herders "carved erotic material for personal use and to allay their mutual pain and their emotional and sexual hunger. All indications are that they enjoyed the exercise. . . . After their own names and herding news—including loneliness—this was the sheepherders' favorite topic."

Many of the aspen carvings, however, are starting to disappear. The average life span of an aspen is sixty to eighty years, so many of the older trees carved during the heyday of the sheepherders are dying off.

If you want to check out these unusual tree carvings, the Spooner aspen grove is located off a dirt Forest Service road about 0.5 mile west of the junction of US 50 and Route 28 at Glenbrook. Follow the road behind a Forest Service maintenance building and continue up a steep hill for about 1.5 miles. Stands of aspen can be found south of the road, and the arborglyphs can be found deep inside those groves.

Place Setting for Twenty-Four

Reno

The Keck Museum, tucked inside the historic Mackay School of Mines on the University of Nevada–Reno campus, offers an eclectic mix of stones, fossils, mining equipment, and one very special silver set.

Established in 1988, the Keck Museum, which is open Monday through Friday from 9:00 a.m. to 4:00 p.m., displays dozens of rare and unusual stones, such as opals from Nevada's Virgin Valley and azurite from Namibia. The museum also has the remains of a three-million-year-old mastodon, found in Gardnerville, Nevada, and fossils of ancient ichthyosaurs, uncovered in central Nevada.

But perhaps the most impressive—and valuable—items in the museum are the two dozen or so pieces from the Mackay silver service. In 1876 mining millionaire John Mackay, who earned a fortune in Virginia City's mines, commissioned Tiffany & Company in New York to design and produce a silver service for his wife, Marie Louise. He shipped more than half a ton of Comstock silver to the company and ordered it to make the "finest silver service possible." Charles Grosjean of Tiffany designed a 1,350-piece sterling silver dinner and dessert service for twenty-four. Two hundred silversmiths worked for two years (reportedly more than one million man-hours) to complete the set, which contains 14,718 ounces of silver.

Each piece bears Marie Louise's initials, MLM, and is decorated by hand in rich, floriated designs incorporating Irish shamrock, Scottish thistle, and American garden and wildflowers. The motif resembles the dense decorations used on Persian and Indian metalwork. Mackay purchased the casting dies used to make the service so that it would never be duplicated. The entire collection fit into nine walnut and mahogany chests, each mounted with a silver plaque detailing its contents.

In 1955 the Mackay family donated fifty-five pieces to the University of Nevada–Reno, which has used them at important school events over the years. In the 1990s the larger pieces in the university's collection were placed in the Keck Museum, including an ornate silver soup tureen; a champagne cooler with a grape and vine design; and a pair of 36-inch candelabra, each with twenty-nine candles, which are the tallest candelabra ever made by Tiffany.

When visiting the Keck Museum, be sure to check out the life-size bronze statue of John Mackay that stands at the entrance to the mining school building that bears his name. It was created by the artist

Gutzon Borglum, who later carved the images of four presidents into the face of Mount Rushmore.

Gilligan's Mary Ann Was Not Really from Kansas

Reno

It's perhaps ironic that Dawn Wells—the actress who played the iconic Mary Ann Summers, the fresh-faced, small-town girl from Winfield, Kansas, on the popular TV show *Gilligan's Island*—was born and raised in Reno, Nevada, where gambling is legal, fast marriages and divorces are big business, and the bars never close. In the 1950s Wells's father, Joe, was part owner of the Thunderbird Hotel, the fourth hotel-casino to be built (in 1948) on what became known as the Las Vegas Strip.

Born on October 18, 1938, Dawn Wells grew up in Reno and attended local schools, including Reno High, from which she graduated in 1956. While in high school, she served as president of the school debate team and was class treasurer. Wells attended Stephens College in Columbia, Missouri; she originally intended to study medicine but later switched to drama. She transferred to the University of Washington, which had a highly regarded theater program, and graduated with a degree in theater. In 1959 she was crowned Miss Nevada and participated in the 1960 Miss America pageant.

Wells moved to Hollywood to establish a TV or film career and soon scored guest roles in shows like *77 Sunset Strip, Maverick, Wagon Train, Burke's Law,* and *Bonanza*. In an interview on a *Gilligan's Island* Web site, she said that she was generally cast as "an ingénue. I played a couple of hookers, but not many." In 1964 she appeared in the film *The New Interns* and was fortunate to be hired for a sitcom about survivors of a shipwreck—*Gilligan's Island*.

Although the show was trashed by TV critics, audiences enjoyed the good-natured adventures of the castaways: Gilligan, the Skipper, Mr. and Mrs. Howell, Ginger, the Professor, and Mary Ann, the role played by Wells. She earned a cult following as a result of the show, which was televised from 1964 to 1967 and for many more years in syndication. In recent years a popular pop-culture game has cropped up that measures personality type by asking, "Ginger or Mary Ann?" It refers to whether you behave like, or would prefer, the sexy actress Ginger Grant or the sweet-natured farm girl Mary Ann Summers.

After the show was canceled, Wells continued acting in touring productions, regional theater, occasional TV shows, and movies. In the late 1970s and 1980s, she re-created her Mary Ann Summers role for several made-for-television *Gilligan* reunion specials and, in recent years, has operated an acting workshop from her ranch in Driggs, Idaho.

So, which is it: Ginger or Mary Ann?

The Fight of the Century

Reno

If you look hard, you might be able to find the worn metal sign in the shape of the state of Nevada on the southeast corner of Fourth and Toana Streets in a rundown section of Reno. The sign commemorates a boxing match once billed as "The Fight of the Century." It stands in front of a shabby wire fence with thin wooden slats, which surrounds a storage yard filled with RVs and other vehicles. The sign, an official state historic marker, says: ON THIS SITE ON JULY 4, 1910, RENO HOSTED "THE FIGHT OF THE CENTURY," A HEAVYWEIGHT CHAMPIONSHIP BOXING MATCH BETWEEN JOHN ARTHUR "JACK" JOHNSON, THE BLACK TITLE HOLDER, AND JAMES J. "JIM" JEFFRIES, A FORMER CHAMPION SEEKING TO REGAIN THE TITLE HE HAD VACATED IN 1904.

Although the site is mostly forgotten, the fight, which became a metaphor for race relations at the time, is legendary. Johnson had become the first black world heavyweight boxing champion in 1908. Almost immediately, many white religious and political leaders as well as sports writers like novelist Jack London called for a "Great White Hope" to step forward and defend the honor of the white race.

During the following two years, Johnson fought a series of "Great White Hopes." Finally, in 1910, former heavyweight champ Jim Jeffries, who had retired undefeated six years earlier, announced he

Fame is fleeting: The site of the Fight of the Century is now a storage yard.

would fight Johnson. Jeffries trained to get in shape, but he was thirty-five years old and nearly 100 pounds overweight and hadn't taken a punch in years. On fight day, the thirty-two-year-old Johnson was a fit 208 pounds, while Jeffries had struggled to reach 230 pounds.

Conducted in the hot July sun, the Fight of the Century was a brutal affair, one that lasted fifteen rounds (of a scheduled forty-five rounds). Johnson was the superior boxer throughout, easily avoiding Jeffries's punches while consistently peppering his opponent with quick jabs and counterpunches. In the final round Johnson knocked Jeffries down twice before the former champion's corner threw in the towel in order to prevent their fighter from getting knocked out. Not surprisingly, Johnson's victory sparked race riots throughout the country.

The fight, which attracted some 22,000 spectators, provided a financial and promotional boost for Reno, then a budding city of about 10,000 residents. Afterward, Jeffries retired for good, while Johnson, a controversial figure because of his flamboyant personality and scandalous lifestyle (in 1911 he married a white woman), continued boxing. In 1915 he lost his title to Jess Willard in Havana, Cuba. He died in a car accident in 1946.

The Reno "Cure"

Reno

When its mining industry began to fade in the late nineteenth and early twentieth century, Nevada looked to other businesses to provide an economic boost, including the divorce trade. In 1906 Laura Corey, wife of William Corey, president of U.S. Steel, relocated to Reno to take advantage of the state's liberal six-month residency requirement for obtaining a divorce. Her stay generated considerable publicity and established Reno as *the* place to get a quick divorce—other states required residency of at least a year. During the next few years, Reno gained an international reputation as a divorce factory for those who could afford it.

In 1927 legislators further reduced the residency requirement to three months and, in 1931, dropped it to six weeks. As a result, by the 1920s and 1930s Reno had become the de facto divorce capital of the world—gossip columnist Walter Winchell called it getting "a Reno-vation." Moreover, Nevada judges didn't require defendants to show cause, which avoided messy and ugly courtroom scenes. The rich and famous flocked to the city to take the "Cure," including writer Cornelius Vanderbilt Jr., playwright Arthur Miller, boxer Jack Dempsey, and actress Rita Hayworth. An entire divorce mill industry evolved; it included divorce lawyers—some pulling in hundreds of thousands of dollars per year—as well as hotels, motels, boardinghouses, and dude ranches that catered to the divorce-seekers. Between 1929 and 1939 an estimated 32,000 marriages were abrogated in Reno.

Newly divorced women are said to have tossed their old wedding bands into the Truckee River.

A popular story that made the rounds was that new divorcees often walked out of the Washoe County Courthouse to the nearby Virginia Street Bridge to toss their old wedding rings into the Truckee River. Though generally considered hyperbole created by Reno publicists, the image of the newly divorced woman throwing her gold band of matrimony from the bridge was irresistible and showed up in books and films, including the 1939 melodrama *Reno,* which begins with a woman throwing her ring into the river.

Although Reno is no longer the numerical divorce capital of America—Vegas grabbed that crown long ago—the city still is a popular choice for those wanting to untie the knot. According to the

National Center for Health Statistics, Reno ranks number one in terms of divorce rate, with 14.2 divorces per 1,000 residents—meaning that a lot of out-of-towners still come to Reno for a divorce. For anyone actually contemplating a Reno divorce, the Nevada State Bar Association has a fact sheet at www.nvbar.org/publications/publications_pamphlets/divorce.htm.

Where Milli Vanilli Tried to Recapture the Magic

Reno

Motorists on Plumas Avenue near downtown Reno sometimes do a double take when they get to the intersection with Mt. Rose Street. There, in the middle of an older, fairly upscale residential neighborhood, is a giant 6,200-square-foot Queen Anne–style mansion that seems to overpower the surrounding homes. Even more unusual is that it's not even really a home—it's a recording studio that gained notoriety in the early 1990s for being the place where discredited rockers Milli Vanilli recorded their final album.

Here's the back story: In 1992 the German rock duo Milli Vanilli decided to hide out in Reno to record a comeback album. Just three years earlier, the two, Rob Pilatus and Fab Morvan, had sold millions of copies of their album *Girl You Know It's True* and won the coveted Grammy for Best New Artist. In 1990, however, they were exposed as frauds when it was revealed that they were merely dancing lip-synchers who had not actually been the voices on their album. Their Grammy was taken away, and the two had become industry pariahs.

Taj, an upstart Reno music label, had recently opened inside a new recording studio called "Granny's House" (now known as Sierra Sonics) at 515 Plumas Avenue. The facility had two full recording studios, eight bedrooms, a full kitchen, and a laundry room. According to Reno entertainment writer Jason Kellner, Taj was trying to make a name for itself and agreed to take on the album, which would feature the real vocals of Pilatus and Morvan. Kellner said that the two

Discredited pop stars Milli Vanilli tried to show they could do more than lip synch in this studio.

spent about ten months in Reno working on the album. During that time, Pilatus, who suffered from depression, tried to commit suicide (he would eventually kill himself in 1998) and would disappear for days at a time.

Sadly, by the time the album was finished, Taj had gone bankrupt, and the studio was taken over by creditors. Moreover, a dispute over ownership of the recording tapes delayed the album's release. When it finally appeared, there was very little interest, and it reportedly sold only 2,000 copies. If you're so inclined, you can actually listen to songs from the ill-fated album, known as the *Rob and Fab Album,* on the Web site Crap from the Past (www.crapfromthepast.com/milli vanilli/robandfablp.htm).

Chocolate Bar

Reno

A warning: If you're allergic to chocolate, don't go near the Chocolate Bar (475 Arlington Street, Reno). Just about every item on the menu at the trendy Chocolate Bar, which bills itself as a bar/cafe/candy shop, contains chocolate in some form. Chocolate-flavored adult drinks? Try the Cocoa Amaretto martini (Absolut vanilla, white crème de cacao, amaretto, and cocoa syrup), the Chaitini (Grand Marnier, Bailey's, and Masala chai, topped with grated nutmeg), or the German Chocolate (Malibu rum, crème de cocao, and Frangelico). A tasty chocolate dessert? Check out the chocolate fondue (creamy, warm milk chocolate with hunks of pound cake, fresh strawberries, and bananas) or the Ice Cream Sammy (vanilla ice cream served between two chocolate chip cookies and rolled in toasted coconut).

The Chocolate Bar, which opened in 2005, boasts that its food and drink are made with a type of gourmet South American chocolate known as Maricaibo, which is processed in Switzerland. To appeal to the true chocolate connoisseur, the chocolate has been rated "Grand Cru," meaning it is of the highest quality.

That's not to say there aren't non-chocolate items on the menu. The bartender mixes a number of tasty fruit-flavored cocktails, like the Blue Sage (Bombay sapphire gin, fresh sage, lime and blueberry juice) and the Orange Pom Cooler (Belvedere Pomarancza, fresh orange and pomegranate juice with a splash of di Soronno). The

Willy Wonka would feel right at home at Reno's Chocolate Bar.

cafe's appetizer list includes non-cocoa stuff like chicken satay (grilled chicken skewers marinated in coconut milk and served with a Thai peanut sauce) and seared ahi tuna rolled in a sesame seed crust.

But the place is called the Chocolate Bar, and it does its best to live up to the name. The interior incorporates dark-colored wood, leather, tile, and other materials in such a way that everything seems like it might be made of chocolate. Small TV screens around the bar often show the film *Charlie and the Chocolate Factory*. So enjoy the truffles, made with chocolate and fresh cream; the chocolate layer cake; or a cup of Mayan hot chocolate, a spicy blend of cocoa, cinnamon, honey, vanilla, and red peppers. If you want a beer that's appropriate for the ambience, be sure to order the Rogue Chocolate Stout—but save room for a slice of the chocolate cheesecake.

Making Lemonade Out of Lemons

Sparks

For more than a quarter of a century, travelers heading west on Interstate 80 knew they had reached the city of Sparks when they passed a big gravel pit. Between 1968 and 1995 the Helms gravel pit, as it was called, provided millions of tons of rock for area road and construction projects. In 1987, however, the pit, which had grown to more than 100 feet deep, was closed when Sparks officials discovered petroleum chemicals and solvents seeping into the hole. They traced the contamination to a massive spill at an oil tank farm located about a mile west. The pit was designated a Toxic Superfund Site, and a major cleanup effort was undertaken. The city of Sparks took possession of the site in 1996, after tests showed that the groundwater in the pit was free of petrochemicals and other dangerous substances. City officials proudly announced plans to convert the former gravel pit into a park and recreational pond using millions of dollars in fees and fines paid by those responsible for the contamination. The original idea was to fill the pit to a depth of approximately 30 feet, which, it was estimated, might take several years.

Then along came Mother Nature. In January 1997 the Reno-Sparks area experienced the highest recorded flooding in its history. The Truckee River overflowed its banks, and an estimated one billion gallons of water poured into the pit. Almost overnight, Sparks had a new body of water.

The unexpected lake, called the Sparks Marina, is 100 feet deep and covers about seventy-seven acres. Ironically, in order to keep the lake at a constant, desirable level, the city pumps approximately 2.3 million gallons of water into the Truckee River every day. Some sport

The Sparks Marina, created by an act of God and landscaped by man.

fish have been introduced into the lake, including rainbow, cutthroat, and brown trout; other species, however, might have accidentally spilled into the lake during the 1997 flooding. In the past decade the city has developed the area around the lake, installing two public beaches, picnic areas, sand volleyball courts, bicycle and hiking trails, and boat ramps. Additionally, the city approved several restaurants and bars, condominiums, and, recently, the construction of a 130-acre, $1 billion shopping and entertainment center that will include a 250,000-square-foot Scheels sporting goods store, a 1,000-room hotel-casino, and a dinosaur-themed restaurant, T. Rex, created by the founder of the Rainforest Cafe chain.

To reach the Sparks Marina, travel east of Reno on I-80 and take exit 19 (East McCarran Boulevard). Head north 1 block; then turn east on Lincoln Way, which leads directly to the lake.

Nevada's Oldest and Most Haunted Hotel

Virginia City

The proprietors of the Gold Hill Hotel like to make two intriguing claims—that it is Nevada's oldest lodging house and that it is one of its most haunted. Regarding the first claim, there appears to be ample evidence to prove it is the state's oldest hotel. The two-story stone hostelry can trace its roots to 1861, when it was built by Louise Forster and Alfred Riesen. Known as the Riesen House, the hotel, according to historian Guy Rocha, immediately encountered problems. In the winter following its construction, severe rains and melting snow damaged a portion of the hotel. By 1862 it had been repaired and sold to Horace M. Vesey, who renamed it Vesey's Exchange (then later, Vesey's Hotel, and then Vesey's House).

The hotel (775-847-0111; www.goldhillhotel.net), located about 15 miles northeast of Carson City via US 50 and Route 342, remained opened during the region's long economic decline, which started in the late 1870s. By 1890 records indicate that its name had been changed again, to the Capital Hotel. Rocha notes that by 1907 it

The Gold Hill Hotel offers good grub, nice rooms, and a few ghosts.

had ceased serving as a lodging house and had been converted into a private residence. In 1958 Dorothy and Fred Inmoor purchased the property and reopened it as the Gold Hill Bar and Hotel. During most of its history, the hotel has consisted of six rooms with a shared bathroom, small dining area, bar, and lobby. In 1986–1987, Bill Fain, who had purchased the hotel a few years earlier, added seven rooms with private baths, a larger lobby, and a small bookstore, as well as a restaurant with a modern kitchen. He also began hosting a weekly lecture series by prominent local historians.

As for the ghosts, the hotel's proprietors insist that at least two phantoms—Rosie and William—have been spotted roaming the

The Far West's First Train Robbery and Lost Loot

It's said that somewhere in the rolling hills west of Reno, near the community of Mogul, a small fortune in gold coins is hidden. Over the years treasure seekers, some even armed with metal detectors, have tried unsuccessfully to find the trove, which supposedly includes some 150 $20 gold coins that today would be worth more than $250,000.

How the coins got there is an interesting historical tale. On November 5, 1870, five masked gunmen hijacked an eastbound Central Pacific train about 6 miles west of Reno. They stole about $41,800 in gold coins and silver bars and then disappeared. Unfortunately for the criminals, the authorities were able to track down one of the thieves, who led them to his coconspirators. Eventually, everyone involved in the robbery was arrested and, except for two who testified against the others, sentenced to between five and twenty-three years in jail.

In addition to leaving behind the mystery of the missing 150 gold coins—which as far as anyone knows are still out there—the crime has lived on because it's generally thought to be the first train robbery in the Far West (the transcontinental railroad line had been completed only about a year and a half earlier).

upstairs rooms. Hotel staff members claim that when Rosie is around, they can smell roses. She is said to enjoy shaking keys, jewelry, and loose change. Her male counterpart, an old miner named William, leaves the faint smell of tobacco. The two specters have gained such notoriety that ghost hunters from around the world flock to the hotel to try to scientifically measure their presence. In 2003 a nonprofit paranormal research group, Ghost Trackers, visited the hotel to film its ghosts.

According to ghost connoisseurs, the hotel's sensitivity to the ghost world is due to its location adjacent to the Yellow Jacket Mine. In April 1869 a fire, possibly caused by a candle too close to a support timber, broke out at the 800-foot level of the mine. Soon flames and smoke filled the shafts and spread to surrounding mines, including the Crown Point and Kentuck. It is believed that thirty-four men died in the fire, most suffocating when smoke filled the underground tunnels in which they were working.

Legend of the Suicide Table

Virginia City

If a story is repeated often enough, people soon begin to believe it's authentic. That's certainly the case with the so-called Suicide Table at the Delta Saloon in the historic mining town of Virginia City, which is located about 25 miles southeast of Reno via US 395 and Route 341. An ornate sign posted above the dusty green-felt table notes that it is known as the Suicide Table because "three previous owners are reported to have committed suicide because of heavy losses." The sign says that the table was originally a Faro Bank Table brought to Virginia City in the early 1860s. Faro is an all-but-forgotten card game, also known as "bucking the tiger," that was popular on riverboats and in nineteenth-century mining towns. It fell out of favor in gambling houses in the early twentieth century because it didn't give the house (or casino) much edge over the players.

The Suicide Table's first owner, the colorfully named "Black Jake," lost $70,000 in one night and then shot himself. The table's second owner is said to have used it only for a single evening, during which he lost everything and reportedly also killed himself (or was killed). The third unlucky owner converted it to a blackjack table, also lost heavily, and ended his life. Reportedly, the ghost of "Black Jake" has been seen sitting at the table, which has been featured on several national television shows, including *Ripley's Believe It or Not?*

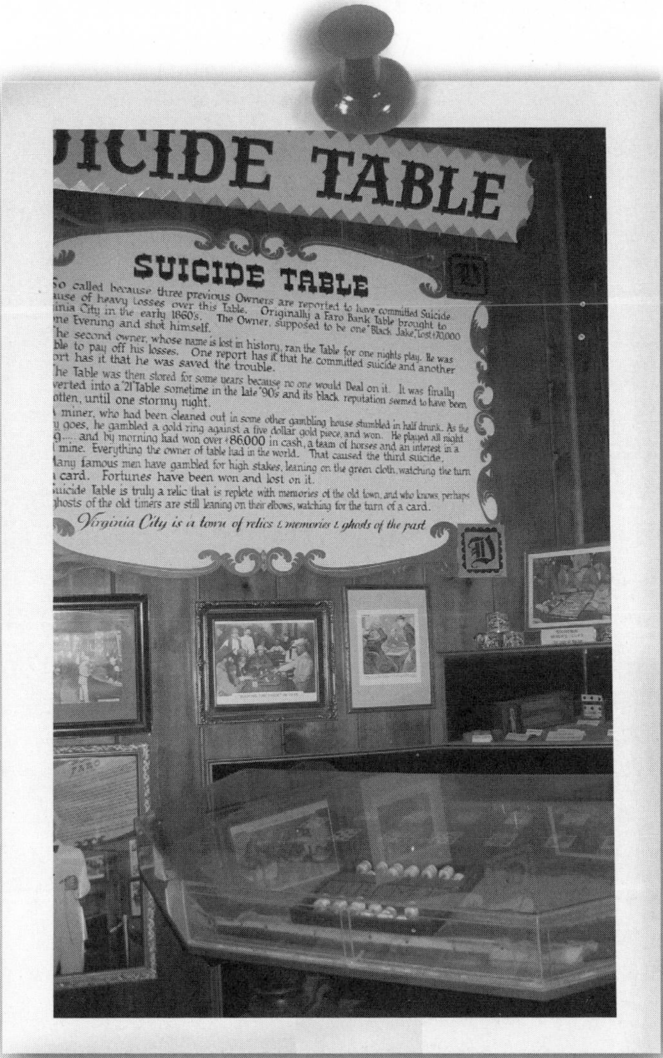

The Suicide Table was for those who didn't know when to fold 'em.

Are the stories about the table real? Some locals laugh and privately will tell you that it's all made up. No one, however, will offer to say it on the record.

Virginia City's Lively Ghosts

Virginia City

For years, Virginia City billed itself as "the West's Liveliest Ghost Town." So it's logical that the former mining town, which generated an estimated $400 million in high-grade silver during its heyday, would be the focus of many ghost stories. In fact, there are at least two books that cover the subject, including *Haunted Nevada* by Janice Oberding and *Comstock Phantoms* by Brian David Bruns.

Reportedly, specters have been seen in about a dozen places in Virginia City, including the St. Mary's Art Center, which is housed in the former St. Marie Louise Hospital. It was built in 1876 and was operated for several decades by the Sisters of Charity religious order. Witnesses have reported seeing a woman in long, white robes or a nun dressed in white robes roaming the hallways and looking out the windows of the four-story brick structure. One version of the story is that in 1878 a patient in the psychiatric ward started a fire that killed him and a nun on duty. It is said that she continues to wander the building looking for patients to help and frequently musses the sheets and blankets on the bed in her former room.

There have also been reports of the ghost of a blonde-haired woman in the spiral staircase near the back of the Old Washoe Club bar. Opened in the 1870s, the Old Washoe Club was originally known as the Millionaires Club and was a men's drinking establishment for the Comstock's most successful business owners. The winding staircase served as the original entrance to the Millionaires Club, which was upstairs. The club offered gambling, prostitutes, and liquor to its members. In addition to the female ghost, affectionately called Lena by regular bar patrons, there have been sightings of an ethereal old prospector sitting at one of the barstools, as well as the ghost of a thirteen-year-old girl, who some believe was murdered in an upstairs bedroom. People have also reported bar glasses falling from shelves for no reason, doors that lock and unlock, and a chandelier that moves by itself.

Beware of the ghostly nun said to haunt St. Mary's Art Center.

Other ghost sightings have occurred in Virginia City's Silver Terrace Cemetery, where people claim to have witnessed a strange glowing tombstone at night, and the Fourth Ward School in South Virginia City, allegedly home to "Miss Suzette," a ghost who walks across the schoolyard to the front steps and then disappears. She is believed to be the ghost of a teacher who worked at the school in 1908.

Some people have also reported seeing the ghost of Henry Comstock, one of the founders of Virginia City and namesake for the Comstock Lode. Comstock is said to haunt the old Ophir Mine, located south of the Virginia City cemeteries (near the intersection of Carson Street and Cemetery Road). According to one Web site (Haunted Hotspots), in the winter of 1874 an odd and mysterious light suddenly emanated from the mouth of the mine and rose 60 feet in the air. Thinking it was an underground fire, several townspeople investigated but found no flames or smoke. Afterwards, there were unusual occurrences at the mine—elevator cages summoned when no one was there—as well as strange noises. Eventually, the decayed ghost of Comstock appeared, identified himself, and said he was reclaiming his mine. Allegedly, he tormented miners by blowing out their candles and howling loudly. The reason for Comstock's restlessness is monetary: He was an early owner of a portion of the fabulous silver vein that bears his name, but he sold his holdings for far less than they were worth (supposedly about $11,000). Later, he tried operating several dry-goods stores; however, he wasn't much of a businessman and went broke. In September 1870, while prospecting in Montana, he allegedly committed suicide. Now, he is said to haunt his former digs.

Racing Camels and Mobile Commodes

Virginia City

Each fall, the old mining town of Virginia City holds two rather unique races—one involves smelly, ill-tempered, spitting camels, while the other features outhouses on wheels. Former Virginia City resident Mark Twain, who enjoyed a good laugh, no doubt would be proud.

The annual Virginia City Camel Races, held over three days in early September, draw 25,000 to 30,000 spectators, all eager to see whether the jockeys can manage to hang on to the untrained camels long enough to finish the race. The event usually includes 100-yard

Photo courtesy of the Nevada Commission on Tourism

Spit happens at the annual Virginia City International Camel Races.

dashes on a straight dirt track. Over the years organizers have also added races with other exotic animals, such as ostriches, emus, and bulls. Periodically, riders from Australia—another country where camel races are held—compete for a 4-foot-tall trophy called the International Camel Cup.

Perhaps even more unusual are the World Championship Outhouse Races, held the first weekend in October. Since the early 1990s Virginia City has hosted the oddball competition, which attracts a wide variety of mobile outhouse designs and shapes, many built specifically for the races. The winner of the double elimination race receives the Royal Flush Trophy, which is shaped like a glass outhouse. Runners-up receive prizes such as a toilet seat and a bedpan. According to organizers, the races were created to honor an episode in Virginia City's colorful past, when the county banned the use of outhouses in the town, leading many residents to put their outhouses on wheels and parade them on the main street.

The race crew can have three members, "all of whom should be of basic humanoid ancestry," meaning that no dogs or other animals can ride in the outhouse. The team consists of two designated pushers and a driver-rider, who must remain inside during the entire race. The outhouses must be pushed or pulled during the 2-block race only by human power, and outhouses must remain in their designated lane for the duration of the race.

In recent years, winners have coasted to victory in mobile privies with names like "The Urinator," "Stool Shed," "Flaming Butt Hut," and "The Golden Throne." In 2006 the latter ousted the previous four-time winner, "The Urinator," in a close race. The event, held on C Street in the center of town, attracts several thousand spectators each year.

The Camel Races actually began as a joke. In 1959 Bob Richards, editor of Virginia City's *Territorial Enterprise* newspaper, published the results of local camel races. The only problem was that there had been no such races. He had concocted the idea of camel races because, for a brief time in the early 1860s, Virginia City had been home to a couple of camel freight operations.

Richards's story didn't get much reaction from locals, who were accustomed to his quirky sense of humor, but the editors of the *San Francisco Chronicle* picked up the story. A year later, Richards again announced the nonexistent event, but this time the *Chronicle* responded by announcing that it had hired several camels and was challenging all comers to a race. Not to be outdone, the *Phoenix Gazette* and the Indio, California, Chamber of Commerce accepted the challenge, and suddenly the fictitious race became a reality. The San Francisco Zoo provided additional camels, and a "ringer" jockey—director John Huston, who was in the Reno area filming *The Misfits,* with Clark Gable and Marilyn Monroe—was brought in to publicize the event. The races were held, and Huston beat all comers.

Since then, Virginia City has continued to host the races during the first weekend in September following Labor Day. For more information about either event, contact the Virginia City Convention and Tourism Authority (800-718-7587; www.visitvirginiacitynv.com).

Not-So-Blind Justice

Virginia City

The gold-colored statue of Lady Justice on the Storey County Courthouse in Virginia City doesn't wear a blindfold. Some of the local tour guides like to claim that the sighted icon, erected in 1877 and made of zinc, is the only one or two like it in the country. The truth, however, is somewhat different: although she may be nontraditional or unusual, she's not all that rare.

Nevada State Historic Preservation Officer Ronald James, author of *Temples of Justice: County Courthouses in Nevada,* noted that there are at least twenty similarly sighted statues of Justice in various countries. Moreover, James disputes the notion that the un-blindfolded Justice was a statement about the nature of western frontier justice. His research uncovered that the Storey County Commission specifically wanted an un-blindfolded Justice for the courthouse, which was built in 1876–1877 to replace one that burned in the Great Fire of 1875 that destroyed most of Virginia City.

James wrote that dating back to Greek and Roman times, "Justice was a virgin with an unerring instinct for fairness. She did not need a blindfold." He said that the image of a blind Justice actually began to appear in about the sixteenth century, when German artists, protesting the unfairness of their country's courts, began portraying her as blind and "staggering" around a courthouse. Ironically, the parody of Lady Justice eventually became her standard image. James, however, points out that "some artists have rejected it. After all, if Justice is truly just, she need not be blind."

Nevada State Archivist Guy Rocha has also written about the statue, in his "Historical Myth of the Month" column. According to

In Virginia City, Lady Justice has her eyes on you.

Rocha, newspaper reports from the time, including the *Gold Hill News,* said, tongue-in-cheek, that the facade of the new courthouse would "be ornamented by a figure representing Justice. . . . In the drawing she is represented without her eyes being blindfolded, which may be

The Mountain Oyster Fry

Sometimes there is no accounting for taste. Literally. While some towns are content to host simple rib cook-offs or chili contests, Virginia City is home to the annual Mountain Oyster Fry, which most locals prefer to call the "Testicle Festival." Each March, teams of contestants, known as Gonadologists, cook up sheep testicles in a variety of dishes. Started in 1991, the event attracts as many as two dozen teams of cooks from around the country who prepare tasty testicular treats. The rules are pretty simple—each team must cook up at least twenty pounds of mountain oysters, and all cooking must be done in the parking lot of the Bucket of Blood saloon, without the advantage of electrical plug-ins. Chefs can prepare them in any style, using any sauce or garnish.

A panel of judges samples the creatively concocted cojones and pronounces winners in categories such best overall taste, most creative use of flavors, best booth, best first-time cook, and best presentation. The event attracts about 12,000 spectators, many of whom wander the booths, sampling the wares. Reflecting the flavor of the event, teams have colorful names such as "Clammy Balls," "Galletti's Gonads," "Great Balls of Fire," and the "McCastrate Sisters." Dishes have included Oyster Po' Boys, Euniuch Nachos, lamb nut chowder, and coconut curry balls. Yum, yum.

For more information about this delectable event, contact the Virginia City Convention and Tourism Authority (800-718-7587; www.visitvirginiacitynv.com).

objected [to] by some as unconventional, but when one considers that this representative dispenser of awards and punishments will be compelled to stand out and take all the sand thrown in her eyes by the Washoe zephyrs, it will be readily conceded that her eyesight would not last long enough for her to get so much as a glimpse of the great wealth to be obtained by wickedly swaying the scales of Right and Wrong. It makes but little difference whether the blind is on or off."

The Storey County Courthouse is located at 12 South B Street in Virginia City. It is open from 8:00 a.m. to 5:00 p.m., Monday through Friday.

Settling Elections the Old-Fashioned Way

As modern as the state gets, Nevada retains a wide-open, frontier mentality in other ways. For instance, the winner of a tie vote in local elections is still determined as it was a century ago—by playing high card. State law actually says that a tie election must be resolved by drawing lots, but the preferred method of deciding a winner is to have the candidates draw cards from a deck, with the holder of the highest card winning the race.

The most recent election decided in this decidedly old-style fashion was the 2004 race for the White Pine County Commission in eastern Nevada. On November 2, candidates Ray Urrizaga and Bob Swetich each received 1,847 votes for a four-year term on the county commission. Two days later, the two met in the annex to the county courthouse. Seated before Deputy District Attorney Kevin Briggs and White Pine County Clerk Donna Bath, the opponents watched Briggs shuffle a deck of cards bought the day before at the local variety store. After explaining the basic rules (no jokers, aces high, top suit is spades followed by diamonds, clubs, and hearts), Briggs cut the cards and then spread them face down in front of the two men. According to newspaper reports, Urrizaga said, "Let the good Lord decide," and drew the queen of clubs. Swetich followed, pulling the seven of diamonds. And with that, the seventy-eight-year-old Urrizaga won the election. The two stood, shook hands, and smiled for the local media and a handful of onlookers. It sure beats settling things with a gunfight.

index

index

index

about the author

Richard Moreno is the author of eight Nevada-related books and was the longtime publisher of *Nevada Magazine*. In 2007, he was honored with the Nevada Writers Hall of Fame Silver Pen Award. He currently serves as director of student publications at Western Illinois University but makes regular visits to the Silver State. He resides in Macomb, Illinois, with his wife and two children.